Unsolved Murders in and Around Derbyshire

TRUE CRIME FROM WHARNCLIFFE

Foul Deeds and Suspicious Deaths Series

Barking, Dagenham & Chadwell Heath
Barnsley
Bath
Bedford
Birmingham
Black Country
Blackburn and Hyndburn
Bolton
Bradford
Brighton
Bristol
Cambridge
Carlisle
Chesterfield
Colchester
Coventry
Croydon
Derby
Dublin
Durham
Ealing
Folkestone and Dover
Grimsby
Guernsey
Guildford
Halifax
Hampstead, Holborn and St Pancras
Huddersfield
Hull

Leeds
Leicester
Lewisham and Deptford
Liverpool
London's East End
London's West End
Manchester
Mansfield
More Foul Deeds Birmingham
More Foul Deeds Chesterfield
More Foul Deeds Wakefield
Newcastle
Newport
Norfolk
Northampton
Nottingham
Oxfordshire
Pontefract and Castleford
Portsmouth
Rotherham
Sheffield
Scunthorpe
Southend-on-Sea
Staffordshire and The Potteries
Stratford and South Warwickshire
Tees
Warwickshire
Wigan
York

OTHER TRUE CRIME BOOKS FROM WHARNCLIFFE

A-Z of Yorkshire Murder
Black Barnsley
Brighton Crime and Vice 1800-2000
Durham Executions
Essex Murders
Executions & Hangings in Newcastle
    and Morpeth
Norfolk Mayhem and Murder

Norwich Murders
Strangeways Hanged
The A-Z of London Murders
Unsolved Murders in Victorian and
    Edwardian London
Unsolved Norfolk Murders
Unsolved Yorkshire Murders
Yorkshire's Murderous Women

Please contact us via any of the methods below for more information or a catalogue.

WHARNCLIFFE BOOKS

47 Church Street – Barnsley – South Yorkshire – S70 2AS
Tel: 01226 734555 – 734222 Fax: 01226 – 734438
E-mail: enquiries@pen-and-sword.co.uk
Website: www.wharncliffebooks.co.uk

UNSOLVED MURDERS IN AND AROUND DERBYSHIRE

Real Life Cold Cases of the Twentieth Century

SCOTT C LOMAX

First published in Great Britain in 2009 by
Wharncliffe Books
an imprint of
Pen & Sword Books Ltd
47 Church Street
Barnsley
South Yorkshire
S70 2AS

ISBN 978 1 84563 114 7

A CIP catalogue record for this book is available from the British
Library

Typeset in the UK by
Mac Style, Beverley, East Yorkshire

Printed and bound in the UK by
the MPG Books Group

Pen & Sword Books Ltd incorporates the Imprints of Pen & Sword
Aviation, Pen & Sword Maritime, Pen & Sword Military,
Wharncliffe Local History, Pen and Sword Select, Pen and Sword
Military Classics and Leo Cooper.

For a complete list of Pen & Sword titles please contact
PEN & SWORD BOOKS LIMITED
47 Church Street, Barnsley, South Yorkshire, S70 2AS, England
E-mail: enquiries@pen-and-sword.co.uk
Website: www.pen-and-sword.co.uk

Contents

Acknowledgements

I would like to thank the following for the invaluable assistance they provided during the research of the cases featured in this book:

Roy Anderson; Suzy Blake of Staffordshire County Council; Kenneth Harry Bletcher; Hilary Brookes-Pollard; Deirdre Buck from Sheffield Local Studies Library; Clyde Dissington of the Magic Attic, a local history group based in Swadlincote; Ruth Gordon of Derbyshire County Council; Don Hale; Ann Krawszic from Chesterfield Local Studies Library; Tom Martin; Alan Moss of History by the Yard; Vicki Schofield, artist; David Clifford Taylor; Nick Tomlinson of Picture the Past; David Tummon of Sheffield Bus Museum Trust Limited; Paul Williams of Murder Files; staff from Burton Library Local Studies; Nottingham Local Studies Library; and Leicestershire Records Office.

I would also like to thank the numerous newspapers and magazines across the region for printing my appeals for information, but most notably the *Mansfield Chad*, *Nottingham Evening Post*, *Derby Evening Telegraph*, the *Leicester Mercury* and *War Times* magazine.

There are a number of people who have proved to have been of tremendous value in my research who have requested that they should not be named. To those, who know who they are, I extend my appreciation. Many of these include relatives of the victims and also relatives of suspects. I have been amazed at the level of interest that my appeals have generated, especially in the case of Samuel Fell Wilson where many current and former residents of Market Warsop have provided me with new information.

Countless numbers of people from local studies libraries and newspaper companies who tried searching, without success, for newspaper articles on my behalf. My thanks are extended to them all.

Finally, and most importantly of all, I would like to thank Brian Elliott and the staff at Wharncliffe Books for bringing this book to life.

Introduction

T here is no such thing as the perfect crime, or so many police television dramas would have you believe. At the end of the twentieth century a national average of ninety-two percent of reported murders had been successfully investigated, with those responsible for the evil deeds having been convicted. Whilst this statistic might appear to be fairly impressive it shows that even with modern, sophisticated techniques of forensic science, for every twelve murders that are solved the perpetrator or perpetrators of one murder remains a mystery.

In the year 2000 there were 681 murders in Britain, which was more than double the number of recorded homicides a century earlier, 312. Even by 2000s standards, that would have left twenty-five murders unsolved at the beginning of the twentieth century. And that was without forensic science and modern policing methods.

It is a testament to the old fashioned police methods, in the absence of DNA, ballistics, blood-spatter analysis or CCTV cameras, that there are not a vast amount of historic unsolved murders in this country with unknown criminals such as Jack the Ripper gaining notoriety due to the rareness of their acts and the reasonable rarity of their ability to escape the long arm of the law.

Nonetheless, a number of murder investigations remain open and the relatives of the victims continue to suffer unnecessary pain and grief as a result of the unrepentant murderers who have robbed the lives of their loved ones.

Murders are still today quite rare and this was more so for the first few cases contained in this book. For much of the twentieth century it would not be unusual for a police officer to never be involved in a murder investigation. Detectives, especially in the smaller towns and villages, would have had little or no experience in handling such cases and would usually turn to more experienced and better equipped forces, often the Metropolitan Police Force which had far greater resources and

skills than any other in the country. Indeed many of the murder investigations detailed in this book received assistance from the Met, but to no avail. Even with experienced detectives the bulky murder files remain open. According to Derbyshire Constabulary they keep a murder investigation open until there is a reasonable chance that the perpetrator is 100 years old, at which point the files are either deposited at a museum or records office, or they are destroyed or, occasionally, lost.

The following pages tell the true stories of crimes that have taken place in and around Derbyshire. Whilst many of them left local communities in fear, some, such as the case of Barbara Mayo who was raped and murdered in 1970, have horrified the whole country and sparked nationwide manhunts. Many of the examples contained in this volume are of crimes that have been reported upon on a far smaller scale but let us not forget those who lost their lives at the hands of evil.

Read about a girl strangled to death at Christmas in a derelict building, a taxi driver shot dead by his passenger on a lonely stretch of road and the case of a police officer's girlfriend who was found sexually assaulted and strangled on moorland. There is the case of a man whose skeletal remains were found in a field in Burton-on-Trent, with the name of the victim as much a mystery as the name of the person who tied him up, killed him and left him in a shallow grave. There is the murder of a domestic servant at a farm in Rolleston near Burton-on-Trent almost a century ago; and the cases of two men who were shot dead on lonely stretches of road before being robbed by their killers. You will also read of callous murderers who allowed innocent men to stand trial and, in two cases, be wrongly convicted. And there are more tales of unsolved violent crimes over the course of much of the twentieth century.

There are examples of murder for greed, sex and cases where a motive is as much a mystery today as when the police first arrived at the crime scene and as much a mystery today as the name of the person or persons who had murder on their minds.

All of the crimes detailed took place within a twenty mile radius of Derby and offer a fascinating and varied account of real life murder mysteries.

Criminal history has shown that even after many years have passed, killers can still be brought to justice. As an American man I know has frequently told me during my research, justice delayed is still justice. Despite the decades that have passed, let us hope that justice can one day be achieved for some of those victims discussed in this book whose lives have been viciously taken and the criminals who have caused so much pain, if any of them are still alive and have not taken their dark secrets to the grave, be given the punishment they rightly deserve. I believe it is possible that someone reading this book will have information relevant to cases mentioned within. If what follows leads to new information being presented to the police then all the years of painstaking research, will be worthwhile. At the very least, I hope the following cases provide a fascinating account of the unpleasant past as we explore real life cold cases in and around Derbyshire.

CHAPTER 1

'Mexican Joe': Swadlincote

1908

hose drinking in the *Bulls Head* were both amused and bemused by the strangely dressed man who had arrived in the small Derbyshire town of Swadlincote during the cold evening of 28 November 1908.

With his old boots, baggy trousers, wide-brimmed 'slouch hat', his jacket so long that it was just above the knees, the five foot eight, slim-built, clean-shaven stranger who had dark, shoulder-length hair, cut an unusual figure and those who caught sight of him could not fail to stare with curiosity at the newcomer. Carrying his entire possessions in a wooden box and small sack, the man was a strange sight as he approached the bar.

If the man's clothing did not gain their attention then his behaviour, which followed his entrance, most certainly did.

After a glass he had brought with him had been filled, the stranger lifted it off the bar with his lips before taking it into his mouth, lifting his head back and placing it back on the bar, its contents still present. He then produced a number of eggs, seemingly from nowhere, and proceeded to juggle them, introducing billiard balls to further confuse his spectators.

The strange character had, it later emerged, displayed his talents to small crowds in several pubs in the south of the county of Derbyshire for at least a week. He would visit a number of public houses in one village, sleep rough overnight, often in industrial buildings, if he could not find anywhere cheap to stay and then move on to another village the following day. At each pub he would perform the same tricks, engage in banter with the locals and then gratefully receive any money given in a collection from his audience.

After entertaining the bemused drinkers, the surreal nature of the mystery man's activities, having no doubt been made

An artist's impression of 'Mexican Joe'. Vicki Schofield

more so by the ale they had been drinking, the man bade his engrossed audience goodbye before leaving the inn. He returned, however, a few minutes later after eleven to order a bottle of ale, but was refused by the landlord, Edward Wood, because the call had already been given for last orders. Frustrated, the entertainer left for the last time and made his way to George Walton's fish and chip cart, located near Coppice Side, to buy his supper.

Whilst being served his penny fish and a penny's worth of chips, the stranger had a conversation with George Walton and another man who had bought a meal, Billy Whitham. He showed the men a handful of coins, and enquired as to where he might find somewhere to stay for the night. The two men

could only advise that he did not spend the night at Wraggs Brick and Pipe Works, situated just off Coppice Side because they hired a watchman, so if he tried to sleep on the premises he might find himself in trouble with the police. However, the weary travelling entertainer had little choice seeing as though the last tram for Ashby had already left and it was too late to try his luck at the local workhouse. With the night getting colder, the man knew he needed somewhere warm and dry to spend the night. The prospect of imprisonment was not a deterrent. He bade the men goodnight and set upon what would be his final journey.

It will never be known whether, if the vagrant had taken Walton and Whitham's advice, he would have lived beyond that cold November night. All that is known is that at some point in time between the discussion with the two men and early the following morning his life was violently ended inside the brick and pipe yards.

It was John Palmer, the Wraggs watchman, who first realised something was wrong at around 2am but he did not realise exactly what had occurred. In the darkness he could vaguely see the figure of a man, who he believed to be sleeping. He ran outside to gain the assistance of a police officer.

Police Constable Sheldon was walking his beat when he was asked to go to what would soon be recognised as a murder scene.

Wraggs Brick and Pipe Works. Derbyshire Local Studies Library/www.picturethepast.org.uk

'Come quickly!' Palmer had shouted to the constable, who he had spotted on his beat, 'Jackie James is in the hovel. I think he's drunk.' Little did Palmer know of the reality of the horrific situation he had become involved in.

Jackie James was a fugitive wanted by police officers in connection with a recent crime.

Quickly making their way towards the building, Palmer pointed to where the man's body was to be found before repeating his belief that he was drunk. Sheldon must have been pleased to think he had found a fugitive and hopefully be able to bring one case to a close. He would soon realise he would be opening a far more serious case of violent murder.

It was not until Sheldon approached, directing a light towards him, that the seriousness of the situation began to dawn upon him. It was soon clear to the policeman that he was looking at the corpse of a man he instantly recognised as someone he had last seen four or five years previously, but even at this point the officer did not suspect foul play, thinking that the conjuror had simply committed suicide. The man was not Jackie James but was instead a travelling entertainer who Sheldon knew as 'Mexican Joe'. It would soon be determined that this was not a case of suicide and the local gossip that the dead man had swallowed a sword and died as a result would also quickly be rubbished.

The man known to Sheldon as 'Mexican Joe' was Herbert Nottingham Turner who, at the time of his death, was aged forty-five. The man's real name was not, however, known until several days after the murder when his brother John Turner, of Pontefract, identified him following extensive police investigations. Turner had spent a number of years before his death visiting public houses where he would perform magic tricks in the hope of gaining a few coins.

He had worked in theatres and indeed it was an advertisement for Blackheath Theatre, listing a name which could only be partially read, which suggested the dead man could have come from Yorkshire, which was consistent with descriptions of the man's accent, and eventually assisted detectives in determining the deceased's true identity. Whilst Sheldon had known the man from having frequented pubs in

Staveley, which is now part of Chesterfield, the constable had known little about the murder victim.

Turner had at one point been married and settled down but upon the death of his wife he had taken back to travelling. He had come from quite a respectable, though working-class family and it surprised many that he had given up a standard of living which far exceeded that of many Swadlincote people, in order to become a busker. It is deeply unfortunate that his relatives did not contribute a single penny towards the cost of his funeral, which was paid for by a number of Swadlincote residents who had never even met the deceased, and that no one from his family could spare the time to attend the service or burial. No doubt they felt shame towards the murdered man, that his lifestyle smeared their reputation and so they refused to pay their last respects in order to maintain a respectable image for themselves.

Doctor Septimus Palmer, who examined Mexican Joe's body, found a number of wounds on the deceased. It was easily determined that a sharp-bladed instrument had been used to create wounds on the left side of the victim's throat and another wound on the top of his forehead. Furthermore there was a deep incised cut at the back of the neck, which had severed the jugular and two nerves. It was this neck injury that had caused the entertainer's death. There were signs that Mexican Joe had attempted to fight off his attacker: the top of the thumb of his left hand was almost severed, showing he had at some point during a struggle tried to grab the blade. The unarmed, drunken traveller stood no chance against his brutal attacker and death must have occurred very soon after the first injury was sustained because the night watchman heard nothing.

There was no sign of a struggle at the crime scene and no murder weapon was recovered. The Lodge, a reservoir nearby, was drained in the hope of finding a weapon but to no avail.

A trail of spent matches was found on a path along Hill Street into Wraggs Brick and Pipe Works yards. The matches were the same as those found in the dead man's pocket. A local resident believed she had heard someone striking matches outside her home late on the Friday night but she did not hear anything else, or see anything for that matter. No other clues were

forthcoming and no witnesses saw Mexican Joe after he had left the fish and chip cart. Was the victim followed or did the killer just happen to go to the brick and pipe yards for somewhere to sleep and met the strange traveller there?

Police were unsure as to why the crime took place. Even the potential gain of the smallest amount of money can provide an overwhelming temptation to kill. Mexican Joe had advertised the fact he had coins on his person but robbery was seemingly not the motive for this vicious act of murder because, in the dead man's pockets, just under four shillings were found – unless the killer panicked after committing his or her crime.

It seems difficult to conceive that any personal grudge against Mexican Joe had provided a motive, because he had only been in Swadlincote for a matter of hours before his life was ended. He had, however, angered people in nearby Church Gresley.

The traveller had been thrown out of three pubs in the village of Church Gresley in the days before his death, on account of his extremely untidy appearance and his drunken behaviour. He had cursed the landlord and customers of one pub, the *Travellers Rest*, saying he hoped they would all starve in hell. Could someone have taken sufficient offence by his comments to make them want to kill or, at the very least, confront the victim, getting carried away in the process? It is possible, after all, that someone who had been drinking in the *Travellers Rest* may have been in Swadlincote on the night of the murder. People have been killed for less; or could it simply have been that Mexican Joe, in his unusual attire, tempted somebody of a violent disposition to kill for no reason other than he was a stranger and because he appeared to be different? Was he therefore the victim of prejudice and intolerance, perhaps with the added temptation of a small financial gain?

A number of people were questioned in connection with the crime, but no arrests were ever made. A local man had been seen accompanying the victim to a number of public houses whilst Mexican Joe was performing his tricks. The man told police officers that he had left the deceased earlier on in the evening, before he had entered the *Bulls Head*. He was able to provide an alibi and the police were satisfied he was not

involved in the crime. Two strangers who had been seen in the *Bulls Head* before Mexican Joe had arrived there were also treated as possible suspects but they too were quickly eliminated.

At the inquest into the death, which opened on 30 November, John Palmer, the watchman, told the coroner that he had first seen the body at around midnight but had not approached because he feared it was the suspected criminal Jackie James.

Before adjourning the inquest the coroner enquired of Superintendent Faulkner when magisterial proceedings could commence. 'When we get hold of somebody!' the detective announced, unable to contain his amusement at what he believed to be a foolish question.

Faulkner never managed to 'get hold of somebody' and the police investigation soon went as cold as the night on which Mexican Joe's life was tragically ended, with the murder remaining more of an enigma than the victim himself.

The last official record of this mysterious case is that of the conclusion of the inquest when it resumed on 16 December 1908. The only additional information provided to the court was the deceased's real name. The jury was only able to return a verdict that Herbert Turner was murdered by 'a person or persons unknown'. More than one hundred years later nothing has changed.

CHAPTER 2

Clara Durose: Rolleston

1910

It was in the stop press column of the *Burton Mail* on Monday 4 April 1910 that those living in and around Burton-on-Trent would have first become aware that a tragedy had taken place on a Staffordshire farm that morning. The few lines of text gave a simple description of what were understood to be the facts at that time, with news only having just reached the paper as the First Edition was being printed:

DEATH OF ROLLESTON GIRL

The death took place at the Burton Infirmary today of a Rolleston girl, aged 17, who expired as a result of an accident.

The small piece failed to display the seriousness of the incident and, despite being only twenty-six words in length, it contained three factual errors. The girl was fifteen, not seventeen, she died on the way to the hospital not at the hospital and, most importantly of all, there was no accident involved. It would eventually become apparent that the girl was victim to one of the strangest murders to take place in the Derby area.

Clara Durose should have celebrated her sixteenth birthday in June that year. She was, by all accounts, a pretty and usually happy young girl, a domestic servant at Rolleston Park Farm, a farm so large that it covered 404 acres and had 200 cattle, 100 sheep, and twenty-two horses. It was not until almost a decade later that parts of the farm were sold off to other owners. The farm was four miles outside of Burton-on-Trent, located next to the main road to Tutbury. It was owned by John Thomas Wrathall, fifty-one years old, and his wife Ellen (nee

Rolleston Park Farm, the scene of an unusual murder mystery. The author

Bargh), who was two years his senior. The Wrathalls had lived, after getting married in around 1885, in Burton-in-Lonsdale, where they had their first child. Soon they had moved to Lawrence House Farm in Levens, Westmoreland (now part of Cumbria) where their remaining five children were born and the couple with their four boys and two girls lived together. At some point around the beginning of the twentieth century they made their journey south and took ownership of Rolleston Park Farm.

Clara woke up later than usual on the morning of her death. She began her work shortly before 10am when she commenced cleaning the churn in the refrigeration room of the lower dairy on the farm. This was part of the main building complex, with various other outbuildings and barns nearby and spread across the vast amount of relatively flat land that belonged to the farm. The teenager was soon rebuked by Elizabeth Kate Wrathall, one of the daughters of the farm owners. Kate Wrathall, as she was better known, was aged twenty-three. She had shouted at Clara at some point in time between 10.10 and 10.15am for

taking water out of the boiler. Kate then, according to her later story from which she never altered, returned to the scullery to continue cleaning.

A few minutes after Kate's departure, a farm apprentice named Cyril Bernard claimed to have spoken briefly to Clara. He thought the brief conversation took place at around 10.15am after which he headed to the kitchen where Mrs Wrathall had just arrived and had started to serve breakfast. After speaking with his mistress for a few minutes he asked where Mary Wrathall, another of the owners' daughters, who was aged twenty-one, might be. Mrs Wrathall did not know. He then began looking for Mary, who had been heard talking to Clara at approximately 10.10am, so she could not be far away, Cyril thought.

Cyril headed into the yard to look for Mary. There was no sign of her. He entered the piggeries where Mary could not be seen. He then went to the top dairy where again Mary was not present. His search was soon interrupted as he walked towards the lower dairy. Looking down the small flight of four steps, he saw Clara Durose lying on the dairy floor, her head two feet away from the steps and one of her feet resting on the spindle of a chair which had lost its back at some stage. There was a pail of water nearby. The time now was approximately 10.25am; Cyril believed it was seven or eight minutes between him seeing Clara alive and finding her as she lay dying.

'What's up Clara?' he shouted according to his later testimony at the inquest into the girl's death, but received no answer from her. He then noticed a pool of blood under the girl's head and ran back to the kitchen for help.

'Clara has tumbled and hurt herself,' Cyril told his mistress who followed him back to the dairy. Cyril lifted Clara's head and the seriousness of her wound became more apparent. It was a deep wound on the right-hand side of the head and splinters of her skull were visible. The girl allegedly moved her arms slightly but if she had ever been conscious it would have only been very briefly. Mrs Wrathall began shouting for help and before long the staff present at the farm had made their way to the dairy. While the farm workers began to assemble, Robert Frost, one of the farm hands, walked past with the 'Black Beast',

presumably the nickname for one of the larger horses. Frost had been down to the river a few hundred yards away.

There was a small puddle of water next to Clara but not in a position upon which she could have slipped. It was confined to nearer her head and was probably the result of water dripping from the wet dishcloth which she held in her hand. Others noted the fact that her foot was resting on one of the spindles of the chair which was five feet away from the door leading into the courtyard.

A doctor was sent for by one of Mrs Wrathall's sons, who travelled to fetch Dr Dobbs on a pony. It did not take long for the doctor to arrive and have the girl taken to the Burton Infirmary. She died en route, and was pronounced dead on arrival at approximately 11am.

A post-mortem took place that afternoon by Dr Buchanan, the House Surgeon at Burton Infirmary, assisted by Dr Holford. There were no marks on Clara's body except for the head wound which had caused the death. This wound was one and a half inches deep, with bruising around the wound, which was located at the top of her head, towards the right, and from which the brain was found to be protruding, such was the force of the impact which caused the injury. Contrary to early press reports, Clara did not have a cut or bruise on her breast or, if she did, this does not appear to have been in evidence presented at her inquest.

The possibility that death was accidental was considered. It was said that Clara suffered from epilepsy and that whilst she had not suffered an epileptic fit during her time working on the farm, which commenced on 25 January 1910, she may have had a fit and fallen down the steps near to which her head lay when she was found, or that she had fallen off the chair upon which she might have been standing. It was argued she could have struck her head against the edge of the steps causing the deep and fatal wound. Clara's mother, Mary Durose who lived in Leigh near Stoke-on-Trent and who identified the girl as her daughter, confirmed to the local press that Clara was prone to epileptic fits. Mrs Wrathall said that Clara had informed her that she suffered occasional fits. The *Burton Mail* originally speculated that she might have been carrying heavy pots and

ROLLESTON SERVANT GIRL'S MYSTERIOUS DEATH.

THE MEDICAL THEORY.

The somewhat mysterious circumstances attending the death of Clara Durose, a servant girl of Rolleston, were inquired into at the Union Hotel, Union Street, on Tuesday afternoon, by the Deputy-Coroner (Mr. T. E. Auden).

Mary Durose, of Wittington, Leigh, Stoke-on-Trent (widow), said the deceased was her daughter. She was fifteen years of age, and was a domestic servant in the employ of Mr. Wrathall, of Rolleston Park Farm.

High profile news coverage followed Clara Durose's death as all manner of theories were discussed. The author

suffered a fit, fell and banged her head. Clara was not carrying any pots, but the fact she had a dishcloth in her hand evidently suggested this as a possibility to the ill informed journalists at the time. The pail of water had been placed on the ground prior to the injury being sustained.

Could Clara have fallen down the steep steps and banged her head? The police believed this to possibly be the case at the start of their investigations. Her head was, after all, near the steps, with her feet pointing towards the door. However, it was soon determined her head was too far away from the steps for her to have hit her head against it, and the edges of the steps were seen to be rounded through use over a lengthy period of time. There was no way that the steps could have created a deep and narrow cut such as that on Clara's head.

The inquest was opened on Tuesday 5 April at the *Union Hotel* and was adjourned by the Deputy Coroner, TE Auden (the position of coroner was at that time vacant, awaiting an appointment) until Friday 22 April, for reasons which at that time were not revealed. It later transpired that it was because

the police realised there was more to the case than they had originally believed. The jury asked that the inquest be adjourned until Wednesday instead because many of them were shopkeepers and Wednesday was a more convenient attendance day. Someone was despatched to speak to Detective Superintendent Moss, who was leading the investigation, to see if that date was suitable. The inquest was then adjourned to that Wednesday but as it happened the Deputy Coroner and jury reconvened on 22 April after all.

The date made little difference because the police announced that they were making further enquiries and asked that it be adjourned once again. On Tuesday 10 May the inquest should have recommenced but Mr TE Auden, who had by this point in time been promoted to coroner, said the police still needed more time and that again it would be adjourned until noon on Wednesday 25 May.

And it was on 25 May 1910 that the inquest finally got underway at Burton on Trent police station. Approximately twenty witnesses gave evidence to the jury after listening to the coroner's reading of a statement of identification made by Mary Durose who identified the dead girl as her daughter. Dr Buchanan then gave his evidence to the effect that the theory of accidental death could be ruled out with medical certainty. The wound had been very slightly oval in shape and it was Dr Buchanan's opinion that the instrument used to cause the wound was something resembling a pitchfork. He produced a portion of skull, reported to be Clara's in the media but I would question that. With the aid of a penholder he showed how far the instrument of death had penetrated Clara's skull. It passed into the brain by an inch or so. Buchanan told the jury that a splinter of skull was visible at the base of the hole and that small amounts of bone were found around the wound. His post-mortem concluded that this wound had caused death and that there had been a small amount of haemorrhaging on the brain. He informed the coroner and jury that he had examined the dairy and had found nothing within that room that could have caused the fatal injury. The item that killed Clara Durose was therefore not something that she could have innocently fell upon, he said.

Dr Holford corroborated Buchanan's evidence and similarly said that he was confident that Clara did not die accidentally. He believed it might have been possible for Clara to have moved a very short distance after sustaining the head injury but that would have amounted to simply rolling over. She would have been unconscious within a very short space of time, he said, suggesting to me that if Clara was seen by Cyril, moving her arms, she must have been attacked immediately beforehand.

The medical evidence was compelling. Following a six and a half hour review of the evidence and a closing speech by the coroner in which he said he hoped the jury would return a verdict that this was no accident, the jury began their deliberations. After only twenty minutes the jury returned a verdict that Clara Durose was murdered by a person or persons unknown. Mr TE Auden thanked the jurors and dismissed them from their duties before recommending that the police now treat the investigation as one of murder.

Whilst it has been said that Clara was generally a happy girl, she had reason to be very unhappy indeed as she began her final day alive. It was actually because of incidents the previous day that she had got up later that morning. On the Sunday evening Clara had been pushed over by Robert Frost during an altercation between the two. Upon getting up Clara had run out the house very fast and gone to the home of Ellen Louise Webb, who lived nearby. Webb later informed the inquest that the girl had been so upset that she had told her that if she had a jacket and hat she would have walked home to her mother. She had visited Webb on two occasions that day, each time expressing immense displeasure at being on the farm.

She had run away from the farm at around 7:30pm and did not return until 10pm. When asked about her absence by Mrs Wrathall a flushed and agitated Clara explained that she had been pushed. The following morning, shortly before the tragedy, Mrs Wrathall spoke to Frost regarding the argument. He told her he had pushed her over because 'She is always chewing at me, and I cannot stand it any longer.' By 'chewing' he meant that Clara was always trying to antagonise him and accuse him of things. Apparently, since his arrival at the farm,

Clara had been causing him trouble. He had pushed her because she had accused him of stealing pastry. The incident in which the two had argued, and in which Clara had been pushed, was witnessed by a number of people all of whom stated later that Clara had started the argument and that it had been fairly minor. No one seemed to be aware of other incidents in which Frost had threatened the murdered girl or, if they were aware, they refused to offer their information.

The incident on the day before her death seems to be one of only a chain of many events which fuelled Clara's unhappiness. Indeed she had written letters to her sister saying she hated working on the farm because of the difficult work and also because she was being treated badly. One such letter was dated Tuesday 14 March 1910, just three weeks before the murder, and the contents of which were more worrying than usual. Concerned about her sister's well-being, Alice Barnes went to the farm along with her husband and another man.

During the visit, Clara expressed the fear she had at being there. Alice told her sister to leave the farm but Clara said she was too scared to do so. It transpired that Clara had not received any letters sent by Alice, because the men who worked on the farm would take them and read them. She informed her sister that these men would try and cause trouble to her and hit her frequently.

As it happened, Clara was leaving the farm. She had been courting a man named Wheeler. Wheeler had once worked on Rolleston Park Farm but had begun working on a farm in Tutbury and Clara was due to leave Rolleston Park Farm on the day following her death. She was moving to Tutbury to be with Wheeler. The fact she was leaving was well known to those who worked on Rolleston Park Farm.

However, before she could leave more information came to light about Clara's state of mind and it was this, I believe, that led to her untimely death. Mary Wrathall found a letter written by Clara, which she had not posted. The letter was found the day before Clara died and its contents became known to several, if not all of those at the farm. In the letter Clara had said she was being treated very harshly as if she was 'a dog'.

This was a case akin to those fictional stories written by crime writers such as Agatha Christie or Arthur Conan Doyle. The ingredients of a classic detective novel were all present: a relatively isolated location, the lack of a murder weapon, the presence of only seven suspects, one of whom must have been guilty, no witnesses or at least no one willing to give information against one of their colleagues. Unfortunately this was a case where there was no Sherlock Holmes, Hercule Poirot or Miss Marple. Nearly one hundred years on though I believe I can offer an argument as to the identity of the culprit.

There were very few clues in this murder investigation but the police seem to have had a very poor handling of the case from the outset. The only known facts were that Clara was murdered, that she was killed by one of seven people, that she was attacked between 10.15am and 10.25am with an unknown weapon, that she did not scream, there was no argument heard despite people being nearby, that nobody was seen acting suspiciously at any point in time prior to or around the time of the crime and no one is known to have given information that was considered at the time to implicate themselves or anyone else.

Although John Thomas and Ellen Wrathall had six children, only three appeared to be at the farm that day: James Wrathall, aged nineteen or twenty was not present and neither were his younger brothers John Bargh Wrathall, aged seventeen or eighteen; and Benjamin Edge Wrathall, aged thirteen or fourteen. There is some evidence to suggest James Wrathall was living in Cumbria with his grandmother.

John Thomas Wrathall, the owner of the farm, was certainly not the killer. He was in another nearby town at the market when Clara was attacked. Although his anger and hatred towards the victim was clear following her death, as will later be shown, he was entirely innocent.

Mrs Ellen Wrathall was one of the eight people (including Clara) present on the farm but like her husband, she was not the killer. She was in the kitchen when Cyril Bernard arrived, and had probably been there a couple of minutes. Cyril had seen Clara alive immediately before entering the kitchen and stayed with Mrs Wrathall for a few minutes before finding

Clara's dying body, although there was a gap of a few minutes. Mrs Wrathall was still present in the kitchen when Cyril returned to raise the alarm, in the process of serving breakfast, a task which she had been carrying out for the previous few minutes. Mrs Wrathall could not have left the kitchen and therefore can be eliminated.

One of the sons of Mr and Mrs Wrathall is the next suspect to be considered. Thomas Wrathall, aged fifteen or sixteen, had been present when Clara had been pushed, the evening before her death. He blamed Clara for having caused trouble on the farm, much to the anger of the coroner who exclaimed, 'You all seem to blame poor Clara, who is not here to speak for herself.' There was no evidence that Thomas had any particular ill feeling towards Clara, above and beyond any general dislike for the girl, and it seems he was dealing with the animals at the time of the attack, although the 'beast shed' in which he was, was only a stone's throw away from the lower dairy on the courtyard and could be accessed through the dairy door leading onto the courtyard and which, according to some witnesses, was open at the time of the attack. It seems likely that Thomas Wrathall did not kill Clara Durose.

There was an employee called Radford, of which little reference is made in the press coverage of the case. On the limited amount of information provided it seems he was too far away on the farm to have been able to get to and leave the dairy in the time available. He can be eliminated.

Kate Wrathall had argued with Clara only a matter of minutes before the attack. Indeed she had rebuked Clara for drawing water out of the boiler at approximately between 10:10am and 10.15am, no more than ten minutes before the attack. She claimed to have been in the scullery after speaking to Clara until she heard her mother shouting, by which point in time the killer had struck. There was no evidence proving her exact whereabouts during the approximately ten minutes between her argument and the crime but Cyril would have passed by the scullery on his way to speak to Mrs Wrathall, having spoken briefly to Clara in between. She was in the scullery at that time and she would have been seen by Mrs Wrathall in the kitchen, if she had left.

The prime suspect was always Robert Frost who had pushed Clara over the previous day and who had upset her so much that she would have gone home to her mother if only she had a hat and jacket. However, although there had always been problems between Clara and Frost, Clara's main problem was with Mrs Wrathall and Kate Wrathall. Indeed her letters to her sister had always referred to Mrs Wrathall and 'Miss Kate'. To my knowledge there was no reference of Robert Frost in them, although Clara had referred to the 'lads' to her sister, when the sister visited. That is not to reduce the significance of any amount of animosity between the two; Clara had accused Frost of stealing pastry and he had vowed to not put up with her 'chewing' any longer. She had also complained about Frost for not having brought in coal on one occasion which had caused greater problems between the two and she had run away from the farm briefly due to his actions only hours before the attack on her. Thomas Wrathall played down any suggestion that Frost hated Clara sufficiently to kill her. 'They were never friends, were they?' the coroner had asked him. 'Oh yes, they only quarrelled sometimes,' he had responded. The coroner also asked 'Didn't you tell the Superintendent of police that these two were never friendly, and that he was constantly threatening her?' to which Thomas responded, 'I only heard him threaten her once about the coal. That was the only time I heard him quarrel with her.' That was a lie though because he was present when Frost pushed Clara on the evening before she died. It seems many people were willing to lie in order to protect Frost, by toning down suggestions that he and Clara hated one another.

It is understandable why the police and others who were observing the investigation through the local press, may have regarded Frost as the most likely culprit, though the police themselves recognised the shortcomings in the case against him, having never actually arrested him. If I was a detective working on this case I would be entirely confident that Robert Frost played no part in the murder of Clara Durose. He was with the 'Black Beast' which he had taken to the river and he only came back several minutes after the attack. His presence down at the river cannot realistically be disputed. Immediately

before he set off for the river, he was with Thomas Wrathall and he was seen arriving back once Clara had been found on the dairy floor. However, the detectives' focus on this man seemingly prevented them from seeing what would otherwise have been a far more compelling lead.

Mary Wrathall had rebuked Clara for taking water from the boiler as had her sister, Kate. Mary had shouted at the servant and then later saw her do it again approximately twenty minutes before she heard that the crime had taken place, according to her inquest testimony. This would mean she was with Clara at around 10.10am which is when she was heard speaking with Clara. Following her rebuke of the teenager, Mary went to the larder and then to the orchard to pick apples, or at least that is the account she offered to the inquest. There is no evidence to suggest she was at the orchard. Indeed when she was shouted to by her mother, allegedly twenty minutes after leaving Clara, she was at the piggeries. Perhaps she was on her way to the orchard but she had not reached there. It was at the piggeries that she dropped her basket in which she used to collect her apples and it was that basket which was later found to have traces of blood upon it. The basket containing the blood was certainly the one with which Mary had been using to collect apples, she admitted as much at the inquest.

If Mary had been to the larder, presumably to collect the basket, and had then headed to the piggeries, then why did Cyril not see her when he looked around the piggeries for her at between approximately 10.20am and 10.25am? Even if she was in the orchard he would have seen her if he was deliberately looking. The orchard was only very small with only a few trees and was only a stone's throw from the piggeries. I believe Mary was elsewhere and ended up at the piggeries after Cyril had been there. Of course, Cyril did not see Mary between the piggeries and the lower dairy, suggesting that Mary could not have been at the dairy whilst Cyril was searching for her. However, the murder had already been committed and there was a murder weapon to dispose of and that is where she could have been.

Of course the discussion of her movements and why she was not seen at the piggeries until after the murder is merely speculation. The facts are that her basket contained blood that

she could not account for, although she did say the basket was not found until two days after the murder but how it could have innocently got onto a basket that, if Mary's account was truthful, would never have been near the dairy is beyond me. No tests were carried out on the blood but because it was only taken from the larder a few minutes before the crime, and it had no blood upon it at that time, and a few minutes after the crime it was left untouched in the piggeries, there can be no doubt that it was Clara's blood upon the basket.

Mary had motive to kill Clara. It was Mary who searched through Clara's belongings to find the letter in which the victim described her treatment as being like she was a dog. It was Mary who went to a Mrs Chester and said that she would 'give it' to Clara. Asked to explain this to the inquest jury, Mary said that by 'give it' she had meant she would give her 'a good talking to for saying she had been treated like a dog'. Mary was never questioned about how angry she was at reading the letter. The coroner always seemed too interested in the evidence against Frost to give any real credence to the theory that someone else could have been responsible and as such Clara Durose's killer got away with murder.

Mary Wrathall informed Mr and Mrs Hamilton that Frost was innocent and she was scared he was going to be imminently arrested. At the inquest Mary told the coroner that she knew Frost had not killed Clara for the sole reason that, 'Because he helped in every way. He carried the water, and did everything he could.' So, because he was a good worker, that meant he could not have killed Clara Durose? Mary had no idea that Frost was at the river when the killer struck. She had taken several minutes to arrive at the dairy after being called for, despite being less than one hundred metres away if her account is true. Indeed her mother had to go and look for her. Maybe Mary was so convinced he was innocent, when everyone believed he was going to be imminently arrested, because she was really responsible.

The evidence certainly points more strongly towards Mary than it does towards Frost, who must have endured a lifetime of suspicion. I believe, however, that Mary may have had some assistance.

Cyril Bernard found Clara whilst looking for Mary. Unfortunately the reason why he was looking for Mary was never revealed which in my opinion is a major oversight on the part of the coroner and police. The reasons why I believe Cyril may have played a role were firstly that he claimed he saw Clara moving her arms but she must have lost consciousness within seconds of being struck. Even if Clara did somehow manage to move her arms a few minutes after the attack, I think he was involved also because he seemingly had access to a pitchfork. It was a pitchfork that Dr Buchanan thought was used in the murder. Employees on the farm said there was a pitchfork in the shed in which Thomas Wrathall and Robert Frost had been working but that it had not been used in a long time. However, Thomas had not seen the pitchfork that morning. The last person in the barn before those two men used it, was Cyril Bernard. He was, it emerged, the last person to have used the pitchfork but he claimed he did not know where he had put it. Again such a crucial potential lead was never followed. No further questions were asked of Cyril regarding this pitchfork and it was accepted that he had used it, put it somewhere and that he did not remember what he had done with it. It seems suspicious that someone should use a pitchfork, conveniently not know where he put it, and that pitchfork went missing on the same day that a murder caused by a pitchfork, or similar implement, was carried out. Was Cyril innocent, was he involved in the crime, or did he try and help cover Mary's tracks? I do not believe Cyril committed the crime itself. After speaking with Clara he went to talk with Mrs Wrathall. He had no weapon with him when speaking to his mistress and he left in a different direction to where Clara was.

It seems unbelievable that someone would kill Clara Durose when everyone knew she was leaving the next day. Would it not be so much easier to just let her go?

Mrs Wrathall told the *Burton Mail* she did not mistreat the girl and she also rubbished the idea that any murder had taken place. 'Why did the gentlemen on Wednesday last ignore the lever which lifts the latch?' She also asked why Dr Dobbs who attended the scene soon after the incident, while Clara was present, and a Mrs Hamilton who Clara had better relations

with and may have spoken to about her problems, were not called as witnesses to the inquest.

Following the crime everyone closed ranks and portrayed Clara in the worst possible light, with a campaign of misinformation. Mr Wrathall told the local paper that Clara was too fond of men and had to be kept away from them, which was totally untrue. She was described as being deceitful, having lied about not going to church on the morning before her death. She was sent to go to church but allegedly was seen going to a friend's house where she was seen by some unknown prying witness, to drink a glass of stout. She was described as someone in the best of health, who was looked after by the Wrathalls rather than treated badly. She had put on two stone during the two and a bit months she worked there, it was argued. Her unhappiness and at least occasional ill treatment is beyond doubt. She was certainly not treat as well as Mr Wrathall would have liked the local population to believe.

Indeed, his anger and hatred towards the girl shines through in a letter he wrote to the *Burton Mail*, which was printed on Wednesday 30 May, part of which read: 'It grieves me to have to vindicate the seven persons on the farm at the time of the accident. We are compelled ... to "blame poor Clara." Our character has not been spared.' He lashed out at those who tried to preserve Clara's memory and fight for justice for her, saying no one even knew she existed prior to 4 April but that there were now plenty of 'champions' for her name.

Mr Wrathall constructed a theory to try and clear his family's name. He said Clara had been cleaning the churnel, bending down and the wind had blown the door. Clara had then stood up, startled by the door being blown, and had caught her head on the lever for the latch which would have been nearby and which was 56 inches above the ground and then she had fallen to the ground and 'wiggled' to the position she was found, on the opposite side of the room to the door. There was no doubt the latch had a very sharp point to it which could cause a serious injury. However, there was no blood upon it, no blood anywhere near this part of the lower dairy and, according to Dr Buchanan, the sharp point was far too small to have caused the wound. The police also dismissed the theory. I can discredit

it further, by suggesting that if Clara had caught her head on the lever for the latch and had fallen to the ground before managing to move a short distance, one would have expected her to perform the natural reaction of putting her hand over the wound. There was no blood on her hand and the fact she still had the dishcloth in her hand suggests she was unconscious immediately upon being struck.

John Thomas Wrathall's blackened picture of the murder victim, and his desperate attempts to suggest she was not murdered at all, beg the question of whether he may have been trying to cover up the actions of the killer. If the killer was one of his children it would be understandable, though utterly deplorable, that he would wish to protect the guilty offspring. After all, his family were 'well-to-do' compared with a servant girl who had created, as Wrathall himself had said, a 'stigma' over the family with her claims of being treated like a dog. It would not take a great deal of imagination to see why someone might wish to help cover the tracks of Clara's killer in order to maintain an image of respectability. In a small farming environment, such as Rolleston Park Farm, I believe Clara's killer could not have continued to live in the farm without somebody knowing who was responsible and there can be little doubt that certain individuals closed ranks to protect one another and portray Clara in the worst possible way in an attempt to prevent sections of the public from demanding justice for the poor girl.

It is unfortunate that the police had entered the investigation believing it was a case of accidental death and then had only eventually come to the conclusion of murder, probably committed by the innocent Robert Frost. As such their minds were never fully open to all possibilities and as a direct consequence Clara Durose's murder remains unsolved.

CHAPTER 3

Thomas Ward: Mackworth

1921

T he workers of Bowbridge Fields Farm were in for a shock. One of their number had not been seen for a few days but concern for his whereabouts had only just begun to enter their minds.

William Cope, the bailiff of the farm in Mackworth, approximately four miles west of Derby city centre, off Ashbourne Road, had noticed the missing man's boots next to the door inside a hay bing in which the man slept, two days after he was last seen, but he paid them very little attention. It was not until early in the afternoon of the following day, Tuesday 7 June 1921, that it was decided the barn should be searched in the hope that some clue as to his whereabouts could be found.

The previous day, Monday 6 June, the missing man was supposed to have fetched some sheep and lambs from

Bowbridge Fields Farm, with the hay bing in which the murder took place. The author

Alkmonton but he had failed to do so and was not seen that night either, which was unusual although not unprecedented. The casual drover would often go out after being paid on a Saturday evening and not return until Monday or even Tuesday, although he would almost always do his work on a Monday if he had any to do, according to Cope.

This time Cope was accompanied by two other employees of the farm: a cowman by the name of Frank Birch and a labourer called Alfred Lewis. It was Birch who discovered the body when hoeing back a large amount of hay in the right top corner of the 'bing' (hay barn). The man's clothing was first discovered in hay on the left hand side of the building, where he usually slept. However, the removal of approximately eighteen inches of hay on the right of the bing revealed the left shoulder and arm of their fellow colleague. Birch touched the arm and it was cold. He was instructed to leave the body. It was clear the man was dead and was the victim of murder, even though only part of the body was visible, and Birch was told that the scene should not be disturbed. The tenant of the farm, Mr Arthur Brassington, contacted the police upon returning from Derby market where he had been at the time of the discovery.

James Ward identified the deceased as being his brother Thomas, or Tom as he was best known. Tom Ward was, at the time of his death, forty-eight years of age. A single man, described as having lived the quiet life, Tom had been employed by Arthur Brassington, as a cattle drover, for some years, with conflicting accounts of how long he had been employed, some saying six and a half years, others saying eight or even ten years. Once a week, as part of his work, he would drive the cattle to Derby market. Prior to commencing work on the farm, he had worked at Derby Co-operative Stores following his education at the Ashbourne Road school in Derby. Tom had no fixed abode but, because he was regarded as being a pretty reliable, hard working and decent sort of fellow, Brassington had allowed him to sleep in a hay bing, which was attached to a cowshed. The hay bing was the middle one of three similar bings when approaching the buildings from the drive. There were two ways of gaining entry; there was a door into the yard and a second door at the back. Tom normally used the front

door, from the yard. There was a window at the back but this was always shut and securely fastened.

At the inquest, which was held at the Church of England school in Kirk Langley, with the children having been given an extra school holiday to make the room available for proceedings, Doctor Southern told the coroner (Mr AN Whiston) and inquest jury that death was caused by a fracture to the skull, which had lacerated the brain. The fracture extended across the whole of the skull, extending over the crown from ear to ear, with two small pieces of bone protruding from the deceased's right temple. This injury, caused by a single heavy blow from a blunt instrument, would have caused almost instantaneous death.

In addition to him having been bludgeoned to death, Tom had had his hands and ankles bound by a length of thin rope, resembling a clothesline, which was loosely tied around the ankles but more securely tied around the wrists. His hands were tied behind his back with the same length of rope trailing down to his ankles. The fact the binding was only loose, suggested to detectives that Tom had been killed in his sleep, otherwise he would have been able to struggle free. So it seemed that Tom was a laying, easy target for the killer although it remains puzzling that he was sleeping on the other side of the bing to which he always slept. He was positioned laying on his right side with his back against the wall.

Three sacks had been placed over Tom's head but otherwise he was naked, though it was believed he was in the habit of sleeping naked. One of the sacks was pressed tightly around his nostrils and mouth. Blood on the hay underneath and a clot in one of the sacks seems to indicate that Tom had been struck by the murder weapon before the sacks were placed over his head. This action could possibly indicate that the killer wished to prevent his crime from being discovered and used the sacks to stop the blood from becoming visible and that he hid the body under the hay with a naïve belief that doing so would somehow prevent people from knowing Tom had been murdered at all, or at least provide him with time to either move the body at a later stage or delay the commencement of a police investigation for some other reason.

Or it could have been that the killer, upon seeing the results of his actions, felt guilt and wished to cover signs of his crime out of remorse. It is quite common for killers to cover blood or bodies, without hiding their victims (with their covers being very poor) but instead to mask a corpse or blood so that they do not have to view the consequences of their actions. In effect, they kill but are too cowardly to accept responsibility by viewing what they have done and by covering traces of their actions they hope to ease their conscience. There were also a few bloodstains on Tom's jacket but it did not appear that this was being worn by the victim when the fatal attack took place, with the jacket on the other side of the bing to Tom's body. How could it have got blood upon it when it was several feet away?

The man's head and neck were black from the processes that take place after death. And although a medical examination failed to determine a precise time of death, old fashioned detective work suggested Tom had been killed in the early hours of Sunday 5 June, before 6.15am when Alfred Lewis, the farm labourer, looked in the hay bing and saw Tom's boots just inside the door. It was believed the killer would have needed light in order to treat the body in the manner in which it was dealt with. The only window of opportunity to do this was Sunday morning or Saturday night, it was determined due to the knowledge that the building was used at all other times during daylight hours and that employees of the farm had seen Tom's boots in the exact same location on a number of occasions since Sunday morning. Medical examination added weight to the belief death occurred Saturday night or Sunday morning, although it would later be suggested that with Tom having been naked on a humid night, with alcohol in his system and a severely wounded head, the process of putrefaction by which his head and neck turned black, could have been significantly speeded up, making it medically possible for murder to have taken place any time on Sunday or even Monday.

The farm bailiff who lived on the farm slept with his window open but he heard nothing to rouse any suspicions. This, in addition to the fact Tom was naked when killed, raised the distinct probability that he was killed whilst sleeping.

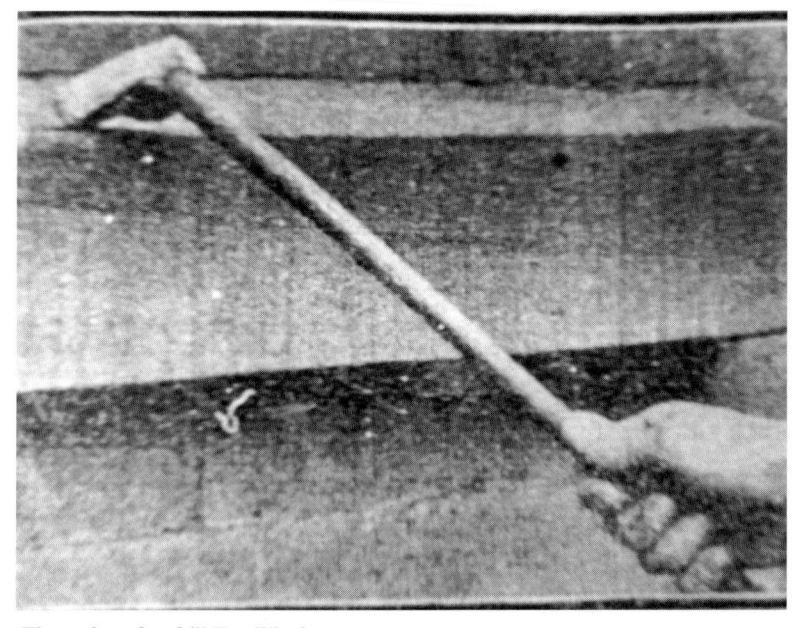

The tool used to kill Tom Ward. Author's collection

The murder weapon was a two and a half foot long, roughly hewn stick of elm wood, which was found in the barn covered in blood and with a human hair, believed to be from Tom, adhered to the stick by the blood. The piece of wood was one which had been seen on the yard nearby on many occasions in the months leading up to the murder, in fact since March. It had always been in the same spot, approximately seven or eight yards away from the bing. There were no noticeable bloodstains on the walls of the barn or anywhere outside of the immediate vicinity of where the body lay. There was no blood outside the building either. This was all further evidence suggesting Tom was asleep when killed and that the murderer had acted with a degree of care when performing the crime. The wood was found a few inches away from Tom's feet.

The elm was quite damp whereas the contents of the barn were otherwise dry and there were no leaks in the building. On the night Tom was last seen alive it rained very heavily for approximately two hours. This led to the suggestion that the murder weapon was brought into the barn following the heavy

rain on the Saturday night and the murder took place shortly after. However, the fact it was still wet days later is not inconsistent with the view it had been brought in at any point after the heavy rain on Saturday.

There was also a cherry wood pipe and a box of matches, along with two old caps, found during the clearing of the barn. These were not believed to have been owned by Tom Ward. Did they belong to his killer? Or did they belong to some innocent individual who might have slept there at some point in time? There was also a walking stick in the bing. Tom owned several, but nobody had seen him with this particular one. Who was the owner of the stick, a stick which only appeared in the building at a time around Tom's death?

A grey-green cap with a big brim, which Tom frequently wore, was missing, as was an old army knife belonging to the deceased, although he had been seen with the knife whilst drinking on the Saturday night, and the police made an appeal for information regarding the weapon, which they believed must have been taken by the killer. Police also emptied ponds, dredged rivers and emptied a reservoir with assistance of the fire brigade. The knife was never found.

Tom was last seen alive on the night of Saturday 4 June, after he had finished work on the farm. He finished work between 6pm and 6:30pm and was paid a £1 note for the work he had carried out that week. He was seen in Kirk Langley, a few miles

Ponds in the Rolleston area were dredged in the hope of finding Tom's knife.
A P Knighton/www.picturethepast.org.uk

Kirk Langley, where Tom spent the evening of his death. The author

north west of Mackworth, drinking in what was at the time the *Meynell Arms* public house, having arrived there at 7.30pm. During their investigation the police discovered the victim had bought and drank six pints of beer and bought some tobacco, handing over his £1 note and receiving a ten shilling note, two half crowns, two 2 shilling pieces and 5d in coppers in change. He left the pub with that amount of money on his person but none of this money was ever found, providing detectives with sufficient cause to believe that the motive for the crime was robbery. Tom left the public house at around 9.45pm in an 'all right' condition, according to the landlord, Mr Geoffrey Taylor.

Later that night, at around 11.15pm, Tom was seen heading in the direction of Bowbridge Fields Farm, by a Mr Charles Taylor of South Lodge, Kirk Langley. Taylor saw the doomed man as he walked past South Lodge. He said goodnight to

South Lodge, where Tom was last seen alive. The author

Tom, who was walking with a 'steady gait', but received no response. Tom was walking alone. There was no evidence suggesting he met anyone and he was unaccompanied in the *Meynell Arms*.

A rumour quickly spread through the shocked community that the murder had been committed by Sinn Feiners, who had been causing trouble at the time. Indeed in the days following Tom's death police officers in London had made seven extensive raids in connection with 'wire cutting', during which five members of Sinn Fein were arrested. The police investigating Tom's death, however, dismissed this possibility as mere speculation by a population that was at the time very hostile to the Irish. Tom had no connections whatsoever with Ireland and it seems he did not know anyone of Irish origin.

Panic and rumours spread like wildfire through Mackworth village following the murder. The author

Rumours of many varieties were shared by the devastated community. Although Tom was a labourer, living only in a barn because he could not afford other accommodation, he was a well-known character in the area and was considered to be a gentle and friendly individual. 'He was the last man in the world to pick a quarrel with anyone,' one of his acquaintances said in the days following the tragic crime. Many other tributes were given in the local press or in the form of floral tributes at his funeral, when he was buried in a family grave at Nottingham Road cemetery.

Tom may have been a gentle sort of man without enemies but somebody had murder on their mind and acted upon their thoughts. By 10 June two men had been arrested but there was only ever one serious, significant suspect in the eyes of the

police but there would never be sufficient evidence, in the eyes of the law, to establish anyone's guilt beyond reasonable doubt.

Police Sergeant Milward was on special duty on 10 June and spent the day searching for a Richard Williamson, who was known to Tom. Milward was cycling along Friargate in Derby at around 5pm when he saw the suspect, who was nicknamed 'Ginger', recognising him instantly by the colour of his hair. Williamson was walking down the street with his cap pulled over his eyes, which, in the opinion of the police, was an act of attempting to conceal his identity. Upon being called to stop, Williamson stood still and waited for the officer to approach him. Williamson was asked to accompany the officer to the local police station on St Mary's Gate, which he did, cooperating fully with the officer. Williamson was not arrested and he walked beside Milward to the station.

Whilst at the police station Williamson was asked to sit on a chair behind a desk near a door. He sat, with Inspector Hollis and Police Constable Wall stood by the desk. The two officers,

The police station from which Richard Williamson fled. The author

10   DERBY M

WHO KILLED WARD?

Resumed Inquest on Victim of Mackworth Murder.

INSPECTOR MERCER'S STORY.

ARRESTED MAN'S BOLT FROM THE POLICE.

Remarkable evidence was given on Monday at the inquest on the body of Thomas Ward, a cattle drover, who was recently murdered at Mackworth—a tragedy which has profoundly moved the whole district.

The inquest was held at the Church of England School, Kirk Langley, the children be-

he could not be depended upon on Saturd nights. His usual way home was across t twenty-acre field. When the piece of elm w first found it was wet. There was rain an or less all through Saturday night.

In answer to the Coroner Cope said th was no trace of blood outside the bing.

however, left after a short time. Police Constable Kilsby, who was also in the room, was busy typing when he became aware that Williamson had stood up. Asking why he had done this, the constable was told by the suspect that he needed to go outside for a minute. Kilsby accompanied Williamson in the direction of a lavatory, at which point Williamson ran as fast as he could away from the station. The alarm was raised and Williamson was pursued by a number of officers and civilians, eventually being caught in Willow Row by an officer.

Williamson had run away from the police but when captured he dismissed the allegation that he had run away in a bid to evade justice. In a police statement he explained his alleged reason for this suspicious behaviour: 'I ran away because they told me there was a gentleman wanted to see me about the murder, and they told me as though I had done it, and I got the wind-up.' The police later denied that anyone had informed the suspect of why he had been brought to the station:

Mr Moore at the inquest: 'Had you or anyone else in your presence told Williamson the reason he was at the police station?'

PC Thomas Joseph Kilsby: 'No.'

Moore: 'Was he told in any way of the death of that man Thomas Ward?'

Kilsby: 'No.'

Days earlier, when a man named Alfred Capewell saw Williamson in Derby market, the former told the suspect that the police would like to speak to him. 'If they want me it's their place to fetch me. I am innocent,' Williamson was alleged to have said, although he did not refer to Tom Ward and so his words could be interpreted in the same way as 'If they want me, they can come and get me. I've done nothing wrong.' Or perhaps Williamson made an assumption that they would wish to speak to him about Tom's death, after all many people knew the crime had taken place. This was deemed an unusual comment to make given that no reference to why the police would wish to speak to him had been made, though Capewell had been told that Tom was dead and he himself had been questioned, as he lay in bed in a lodging house, by two detectives who wanted to know where he had been at the time of Tom's murder.

This suspicious action and other information gleaned during police questioning led police to make their breakthrough and Richard Williamson, of Hewitt's Lodging House, Bridgegate, Derby, was charged with the murder of Thomas Ward in July 1921. Asked if he had any comment to make Williamson simply muttered: 'Only that I am innocent.' When remanded into custody and committed to trial by the magistrates the following day, the *Derbyshire Advertiser* described Williamson as being 'cheerful as ever' as he entered the dock. He was sent to Nottingham Gaol to await his trial.

Despite Williamson already having been charged with murder, the inquest jury into Tom's death, upon hearing almost all of the evidence that was later presented at the murder trial, was unconvinced that Williamson was responsible and it accordingly reached a verdict of murder by person or persons unknown. Despite this the magistrates decided, after discussing amongst themselves for five minutes, there was a *prima facie*

case against the suspect and that he should stand trial at the next Derbyshire Assizes.

Williamson was twenty-eight years old at the time of his trial, which began in November 1921, and he informed the court that he had worked occasionally as a drover. Prior to this he had served in the Army but had been discharged when he contracted malaria. He had received an Army pension but shortly before the murder the pension had been reduced from sixteen shillings to eight shillings per week, providing him with a motive to commit this crime of murder and robbery.

Williamson did himself no favours and put himself in the dock by lying about his movements on the night of the murder so as to create a false alibi. Asked where he was on that Sunday night, he had told the police: 'I was in bed at Hewitt's, Bridge Gate, number 26 bed. I went to bed at a quarter to twenty past ten. I had been at my sister's at 23 Noel Street, from 5pm to 10pm. I had my tea before I went to my sister's. I sat in the hall with my sister and brother-in-law, George Tristram, and another young chap.'

At another time he had also lied to detectives about when he last saw the deceased: 'The last time I saw Tom Ward was Thursday. It was Thursday. He passed me with a pony and float, going up Ashbourne Road at the Derby end, not far from the town. I got in the cart and rode for two or three minutes and then got out and went to my sister's. He told me he had to meet Mr Brassington at the blacksmith's shop.'

Williamson's deceit had been revealed on 12 June during further questioning when Mercer said he knew that Williamson had not been at the lodging-house. 'I was in the lodging-house,' he said defiantly before hesitating and admitting he had lied, 'I admit I was not at the lodging-house. I was walking about the best part of the night. I was at Windmill Lane and the gardens at Ashbourne Road. I slept at Bowbridge Fields Farm on the Friday night, June 3rd. I slept with Ward. I came away from the farm on the Saturday morning. I slept aside of him, him on one side and me on the other. On Saturday night, when I left my sister's, I went up Windmill Lane. I was coming down Ashbourne Road towards the town at 5 o'clock on Sunday morning. There are two hayricks in a field in Windmill Lane,

and I slept between them for about two hours, and then got up and walked about because I was cold. I did not meet anyone I knew.'

On the Friday before the murder, Williamson had insufficient money to pay for a bed in a lodging house, which is why he slept in the hay bing with Tom. However, at 9.30am on the Sunday morning he had enough money to eat breakfast, having been served by Clara Robinson who informed the hearing which committed Williamson to trial that he had handed her a shilling and received 5d change, and he spent Sunday night in the Hewitts lodging-house. There was a clear change in his financial situation following Tom's murder but was this merely coincidence? At his trial it would be argued that he had been given money on the Saturday night and witnesses testified to this effect.

In his statement to the police, Williamson dismissed claims that he would have killed the drover. 'I have never heard Ward quarrel with anyone, we are good pals and like two brothers. I was in the army three years and before I went away I used to work with him droving.'

When first questioned, Williamson had a slight bruise over his left eye; 'I have no idea what it is,' he told detectives, but this bruise naturally featured in the prosecution's case against the accused, even though Tom presumably did not struggle with his killer whilst he was being murdered.

When asked to account for blood on his sleeve he had said: 'I don't know. It might be off my sister's lad, as I often play with him and he may have had scratches.' Again, the jury was asked to consider this to be crucial evidence.

As for clothing worn by Williamson on the night Tom Ward was killed, Williamson had disposed of part of his clothing. 'I have only got this suit and this shirt. I put on this clean shirt on Sunday, and threw the old one away in the dust bin at the lodging-house as it was lousy, and I would not trouble to wash it again,' he said in his police statement.

And did he recognise the elm wood murder weapon? 'I do not know the stick shown to me with the knob at the end. I should think it is maple and has not been long cut. I should think it was cut with a chopper, and it has not long been cut,' Williamson answered.

Williamson, who had worked occasionally on Bowbridge Fields Farm and knew the victim, had motive and opportunity to commit the crime, being able to arrive, stay and leave without raising suspicions because he knew where Tom slept at night and had probably occasionally slept there himself. He told the inquest, upon being asked whether he knew where Tom slept: 'Yes. I knew where he slept. In the bing. The second or third bing from the gate. I could go to it, but I do not know whether it is the second or third ... I know the farm well. I used to work there. I last worked there in 1915.'

He would have known where people slept and would have had a reasonably good idea of how to enter and leave whilst reducing the prospects of anyone being aware of his presence. Importantly, he would have known where Tom slept and it was 'obvious' according to Mr Bendle W Moore, representing the Director of Public Prosecutions, that the killer would have known this fact. That the rope used to bind Tom's hands and ankles together was from a nearby barn on the farm added to the belief that the murderer was familiar with the buildings, it was argued. This is not necessarily true; Tom's killer could have searched through a number of buildings for his victim and happened to see the rope during his search. A farm labourer, Alfred Lewis, informed the inquest jury that the rope could be obtained from the barn without the need to open the door. Also, the rope had only been seen in the barn on the Wednesday, three days before the murder. Its location at the time the killer took possession of it is uncertain. My problem with this evidence is that if the rope was not in the haybing before the killer entered, why did he go to great lengths to find it and expose himself to the risk of being seen? If Tom was asleep it would have been unnecessary to tie him.

There was a dog on the farm for the nine months before the murder and the dog was known to be very aggressive with strangers. Despite being a light sleeper, Mr Brassington did not hear the dog barking and it has already been remarked upon that the farm bailiff, who had his window open all night, failed to hear anything. Williamson was a stranger to the dog, although he had slept at the farm on the Saturday night.

Although Williamson admitted sleeping with Tom on the Friday night, he claimed he did not see his alleged victim

because it was dark and Tom was asleep. Williamson admitted to having slept with Tom on three occasions in the two weeks prior to the murder.

After observing a two minutes' silence, it having been Armistice Day, Mr Healy began his speech for the defence. He told the jury that Williamson was present 'confident under God in the survival of those institutions of this land for the preservation of which in their integrity and in order that liberty should endure those men have passed from our midst.'

If religious rhetoric failed to introduce doubts as to the evidence against Williamson, the rest of the defence's case certainly did.

The defence case was that Williamson did not play any role in the murder of Tom Ward. Instead the victim had met someone on his way to the farm after leaving the pub and that that individual had returned with Tom, or arrived at a later time, having seen him in possession of money, and killed him. The defence believed the killer did not act alone and was part of a small group of people who were able to overpower the victim, whereas Williamson was not known to have associated with anyone or been with anyone after leaving his sister's home.

Williamson told the judge that he did not know Tom to have any enemies and that he had never known Tom to allow anyone else to sleep in the bing. Of course, if guilty, it would have been in his interests to lie about both these aspects of the case.

Williamson's defence were able to demonstrate that someone other than their client had been sleeping rough in the area around the time of the murder.

Mr Harold M Smith [for Williamson]: 'Have you since been making enquiries in the district?'

Chief Inspector Mercer: 'In what way?'

Smith: 'About another man who had been sleeping out?'

Mercer: 'Yes.'

Smith: 'A man who had been convicted for fowl stealing, of this neighbourhood?'

Mercer: 'It would be about four miles from here, at Dalbury Lees.'

Smith: 'You found he had been sleeping out in the neighbourhood?'

Mercer: 'He had been sleeping out in the daytime.'

Smith: 'About the same time?'

Mercer: 'It was a week later.'

The man was a known violent criminal but police investigations suggested he was not involved in the murder of Thomas Ward. Their enquiries seemed to suggest the man went to bed two miles away from the crime scene at 10pm and did not rise until 6am the following morning. Further, there was no evidence that he knew the farm or had ever been there. Yes, he had stolen fowl from a number of farms in the area but there was nothing to connect him to Bowbridge Fields Farm and whilst he had been violent there was no history of violence anywhere near resembling that inflicted upon the murder victim, although Williamson had no record of violence. The prosecution argued that the evidence against this unnamed man was far outweighed by that against Williamson who certainly knew the farm well and had admitted (eventually) to sleeping in the farm the previous night and the fact he had lied at all should weigh considerably against him, the jury were told.

Williamson had a deformity of one of his hands. He argued that whilst he could move a body without assistance, he would not have been able to tie a knot. Of course, the bindings had only been tied loosely around the ankles but even this would have been an impossible task for their client the defence stated.

The defence offered a partial alibi for the jury's consideration. The time of Tom Ward's death was never determined. It could be that he was killed on the Sunday morning during daylight hours, in order to commit the crime without leaving much evidence and having contained the blood in one small area. Indeed the killer would have required some source of light in order to kill, place three sacks over the victim's head and cover

him with hay. The fact none of the farm workers noticed anything amiss in the bing, despite repeated visits, shows the killer covered his tracks reasonably well.

Of course, the killer could have used a candle or other implement to burn for light but there is no evidence for this and there was no suggestion that Williamson had done such a thing. There would have been ash had a stick been set alight to act as a torch.

If the murder was committed even immediately as dawn broke, Williamson was probably innocent. It would have taken him time to kill and prepare the scene but he was in Derby by 9:30am which would have left him little time to kill and then walk to Derby. Indeed the trial judge advised the jury that unless the murder was committed on the Saturday night there was no case against Williamson.

The defence argued that the murder had to have occurred on the Sunday morning because Tom was seen at 11.15pm and he was not even near the farm by that time. They contended that Tom had gone on to drink somewhere else, which he did occasionally do, and that he met someone and quarrelled with them and there had been a fight. This is how blood ended up on the victim's jacket, it was alleged, because the victim certainly was not wearing the jacket when his killer struck. This was extremely speculative argument but the one fact was that if Tom had gone to the farm after 11.15pm and went to sleep before his killer arrived, the chances were that the crime took place on the Sunday, before Birch saw the dead man's boots, without seeing the boots' owner, at 6:15am at which point it is safe to say that Tom Ward was dead and covered by the hay.

And indeed the defence argued that the murder could have taken place at any time during the Sunday because nobody had tried looking for the man until Monday night although he almost certainly was dead before Monday.

So where was Williamson on the Saturday night? His account has already been provided but is it truthful and accurate?

Richard Williamson, the defendant's father, said the accused left 23 Noel Street, Derby (where the witness lived with his daughter) at 10.50pm and returned at 9.30am the following morning. The defendant's father further testified that one of

his daughter's boyfriends arrived with the daughter ten minutes after Williamson left. The boyfriend then, it emerged, had caught up with Williamson and they had walked together.

Albert Henry Ottewell, the boyfriend, a fitter of 4 Co-operative Street corroborated this story. He also told the court that he had lent Williamson three shillings as the men went their separate ways at Ford Street. This is how their client had been able to afford breakfast and lodgings, the defence team argued.

And, speaking of money, the defence asked where was the fifteen shillings stolen by the killer? If Williamson was the murderer what had he done with what for him would have been a reasonably substantial sum? And where was the knife and cap which had been taken by the person responsible for causing Tom Ward's death?

The walking stick found in the hay bing, which seemed to have arrived the night Tom Ward was killed, did not belong to Williamson, who did not own or use such a stick. Nobody had ever seen him with it. Did it belong to the killer and if it did not why was it there? Equally, the two caps found in the hay, neither of which belonged to the victim, seemingly equally did not belong to the accused, or the cherry pipe for that matter.

There was not a lot of blood on Williamson's clothing such that one would expect to find on the clothing of a man who had committed such a bloody crime, although by his own admission he had disposed of a shirt. However, the prosecution argued a small amount of someone's blood was on the sleeve of a jacket he admitted to having worn. This being the case, the prosecution's argument was that Williamson had killed Tom whilst wearing the jacket or he had moved him whilst wearing it. Either way it seems inconceivable that with such horrific injuries blood would have ended up on the sleeve alone and only a small amount of blood at that. There would have been blood on his trousers and all over his jacket had he killed unless he committed the crime when naked or semi clothed. He left none of his distinctive ginger hairs on the body and his fingerprints were not found on the murder weapon, although forensic tests were primitive in 1921 and exhibits were not handled well.

Other than his lie as to where he was on the night of the murder, having originally told the police he was at Hewitt's lodging-house, there was no evidence against him. And this lie could be argued away by suggesting he feared he would be implicated and felt the need to save himself; a foolish, but understandable, action if innocent but a calculated plan if guilty.

Continuing the theme of religious rhetoric, the defence asked the jury to acquit: 'There is one person alone who knows what the truth of this case is and on his word you were sworn to do justice in this case. I call upon you most earnestly to recognise the weaknesses of our common claim, and leave to the eternal justice the final determination of this matter.'

The judge's summing up of the evidence lasted one hour and twenty-five minutes and finished at 3.25pm, at which point the jury were sent out to consider their verdict. It took a little over half an hour before they returned and announced they had reached a verdict they all agreed on: Richard Williamson was 'not guilty' of the murder of Thomas Ward. After months of police investigation it had taken just over thirty minutes for the jury to recognise there was reasonable doubt about the police and prosecution's theory as to the circumstances of that night in the haybing. Half an hour to show that the police's work was not over and indeed that it had to begin all over again. Williamson walked free to continue his life on the basis of serious flaws in the case against him; Tom Ward's family and detectives left with the recognition that a killer continued to walk free.

Whether it was Williamson or another employee of the farm, or indeed a complete stranger, whose vicious actions in the name of greed led to the brutal death of Thomas Ward, what remains certain is that Tom's killer evaded justice and that his murder remains, to this day, one of Derbyshire's most horrific unsolved crimes of the twentieth century.

CHAPTER 4

Samuel Fell Wilson: Market Warsop

1930

It was almost quarter to one, on the morning of Tuesday 23 September 1930, that Police Constable Holland, who was stationed at Rufford, was cycling home from Langwith Fields. He thought his work was done for the night but he was terribly mistaken. As he cycled along Forest Road, approximately halfway between Market Warsop and Clipstone in north-west Nottinghamshire, he saw a stationary vehicle at an awkward angle in the road near the then derelict Warsop windmill on the nearside of the road facing in the direction of Market Warsop.

The spot where Samuel Fell Wilson was shot. The author

The car was just a stone's throw from Sherwood Forest where legend has it that Robin Hood ambushed and robbed from the tyrannical rich and gave to the needy poor. PC Holland had stumbled upon what was to become another story in history of a man being ambushed and robbed, but this time the culprit had no intention of distributing the proceeds of his crime.

The vehicle's lights were not on and, as he approached with caution, PC Holland called to the driver but received no response. He moved closer, still wondering why the car was parked in such an unusual position on a main road and, peering into the window, he was greeted with the most horrendous scene he was to encounter during his time in the force.

The grisly sight of a dead man in the driver's seat, with one hand on the steering wheel and his body huddled up, was plainly visible. The man had been shot in the shoulder and in the face. The wound to the face had been directed at the cheek bone and had destroyed his left eye. It would later be determined that it had penetrated the skull and caused serious fractures. There were no bullet holes in the windscreen or side windows of the vehicle, a four-seater Morris Cowley open-topped car, which had been converted into a commercial van and had its roof up.

The van had a running board on its side and it was, for a time, believed that the killer may have been stood on this, pointing his gun into the driver's window. This theory was never discounted, though emphasis was later placed upon the belief that the murderer was standing on a grass verge beside the road and was a crack shot.

Police Sergeant Robinson of Ollerton arrived quickly at the crime scene by car, followed soon later by Sergeant Holmes of Warsop. The investigation was initially led by the Chief Constable of Nottinghamshire, Colonel Lemon who was under no illusions as to the challenges that lay ahead. Colonel Lemon and Superintendent Neate of Mansfield Police examined the scene and began enquiries in the village.

Several cars travelled along that stretch of road but the crime itself was not witnessed and no one saw anyone acting suspiciously at or around the crime scene before, during or

Market Warsop.

Warsop village, where Samuel was a well respected member of the community. The people of Warsop still wait for new light to be shed on this tragic case. Nottingham County Council/www.picturethepast.org.uk

after the murder. As a result detectives could only speculate about the circumstances of the crime based upon the little evidence that was available to them on the stretch of road where the shooting had taken place.

Tracks on the road showed that the vehicle had come to a halt after having travelled erratically. In the final seconds of the car journey the driver had clearly lost control of the vehicle, causing him to swerve onto the grass verge before returning to the road, before coming to a standstill after sixty yards. It was speculated that the firing of the first bullet had caused him to lose control, with the victim having brought the vehicle to a stop at which point the second, fatal bullet was fired killing him immediately. The engine had been switched off and the handbreak applied. Once he had committed his crime it is

The church where Samuel's funeral service took place. The author

believed the murderer switched off the vehicle's lights and made good his escape.

The victim was soon identified as Samuel Fell Wilson, a forty-year-old provision merchant of 2 Sherwood Street, Warsop, his home being only approximately a mile and a half from where he met his untimely end and it appears he was driving home when he was killed. In addition to being a provision merchant, selling groceries, wine and other products, Samuel had produced the *Warsop and District Almanac*. He was a married man, having been married eighteen months, with a young daughter and was from a long line of Wilsons to live in Warsop. He was head of the firm Wilson and Son, a small but successful business established by his father (who was also called Samuel Fell Wilson and who survived his son by two years). Some of those who remember the crime have told me of their belief that Samuel was also an insurance collector.

Mansfield police station was still being built at the time of Samuel's murder. Investigations began in a cabin at the rear of this building. Ian Brown LPRS/www. picturethepast.org.uk

There was no mention of this in any of the newspaper articles of the time, or the police files I have seen. Indeed the Kelly's Directory lists Samuel as being simply a 'grocer'. Samuel was a very well-known man who was held in the highest regard by those who knew him and by the local community as a whole. His father had been a councillor in the days when councillors were well respected by the majority. Indeed, such was the high regard in which the community held him, that the local church could not contain all those wishing to attend his funeral on 25 September and the churchyard was overflowed according to the local press who said that all the residents of Warsop were present. Certainly, the majority of the village turned out to see the hearse drawn by four black horses, lining the street between the Mill Bridge and the church doors.

Warsop Police had probably never dealt with a murder investigation before, or at least certainly not in recent years. It

did not take Mansfield police long either to realise that they did not have the resources or experience to deal with what was clearly going to be a difficult and baffling case. Therefore detectives from Scotland Yard were almost immediately called in and Chief Inspector Berrett and Detective Sergeant Harris travelled by train, from London St Pancras, arriving on the Tuesday afternoon. Berrett and Harris were amongst the Yard's greatest and most determined detectives; three years earlier the pair had investigated the murder of Police Constable Gutteridge of Essex Police and they had spent 130 hours out of 160 consecutive hours on what was a very complex hunt. A similar amount of effort was to be exerted in the search for Samuel's murderer.

The Scotland Yard detectives looked at the vehicle and fingerprints experts, Inspector Cherrill and Sergeant O'Brien from Scotland Yard, undertook a detailed examination of the vehicle. The science of fingerprints in 1930, whilst very primitive by today's standards, was really quite impressive, with Scotland Yard having 500,000 prints on file by the end of 1930 and there was the belief among the public at large that once fingerprints were found at a crime scene then the speedy capture of any culprits was inevitable, such were the expectations surrounding this form of science twenty-seven years after it was first successfully used in a criminal trial. Fingerprints were found on the gear lever, the switch for the lights, the windscreen and elsewhere inside the vehicle. The van had been taken to Mansfield police station and kept behind the building for further examination, with the body in Warsop's Council Offices where a post-mortem was undertaken.

Scotland Yard wasted no time in their investigation. Two Warsop men were questioned on the night of Tuesday 23 September and asked to account for their movements on the previous night. Neither gave any information implicating themselves in the crime.

On Friday 26 September, the local press had announced that a breakthrough in the murder investigation was imminent. Great emphasis was placed on a report from the fingerprints experts which was due to be received by the investigating detectives the following day. As a result the police were followed

everywhere on the Saturday by villagers anticipating an arrest. Their hopes were dashed and the reason why was printed in the *Evening Post* that day. It transpired the fingerprint findings had been negligible; there were so many prints and it had been impossible to differentiate between them. No decent prints had been obtained.

There had been no footprints at the scene of the crime either. Indeed there were no clues in the vehicle or anywhere on that stretch of road which could conclusively link a suspect to the crime scene if a suspect was identified.

A search of the road, grass verges, hedgerows and surrounding land was undertaken by men in flat caps and trilby hats and raincoats, with sticks, spades or pitchforks in hand; a far cry from today's meticulous examinations with forensic-aware search teams in overalls to reduce the chances of contaminating evidence. Most of the hedgerows and thick undergrowth within a mile radius of the crime scene was scoured for the weapon, as was Warsop Wood, a quarter of a mile away. These searches failed to locate the weapon but they did reveal what was believed to be a clue.

A hammer, believed to be an engineer's hammer, was found within a hedge on the evening of Thursday 25 September. It was found by Mr A Crooks between 200 and 300 yards from where Samuel had been killed. It was five feet into the hedge, had not been there very long in the opinion of the police and it must have been put there deliberately. It had a bloodstain on the wooden handle. How this featured in the crime, if indeed it was connected at all, remains uncertain.

A witness informed police he had seen a man in a raincoat putting something in his pocket. He reported seeing this at 10.50pm before the police were aware the crime had taken place and so they never took the witnesses details and attached no significance to the sighting at the time. The sighting took place near the Cooperative Stores on Queens Street, Mansfield where the man was standing in a doorway. The sighting was reported to a police officer in Mansfield market place.

Another sighting was reported of a man acting suspiciously near the gates of the Duke of Portland's residence at Clipstone following the murder. What was believed to have been a

possible lead, led nowhere. It was not deemed relevant to the murder hunt.

Samuel left home at around 3pm on the Monday in order to collect accounts and orders from the Clipstone district, which was his usual custom on a Monday afternoon. When his account books were scrutinised it did appear that he had only collected approximately £6, which was the total sum of money he had on his person when his body was discovered following the murder.

A nightdress was found in the back of Samuel's van but this was found to belong to Samuel's sister, who had broken her leg and he was taking it home to wash before returning it to her. He had visited his sister earlier in the day.

The murder is believed to have been committed after 9pm on the Monday night. Two children, Norman and Patricia Tattersall, who lived on Forest Road both claimed to have heard the sounds of two gunshots shortly after they went to bed at 9pm. After hearing the shots Norman, aged twelve, had got out of bed and looked at his watch so the time was not in dispute. Another witness reported hearing gunshots at around 9.30pm, however. Nonetheless, the murder was committed at some point after 9pm and probably not later than 9.30pm.

A post-mortem carried out by Dr Wilson, of Church Street in Warsop, on the morning of Tuesday 23 September and initial examination of Samuel's corpse suggested he was killed approximately three or four hours before the discovery of his body. It transpired that in addition to the gunshot wounds, Samuel had had three of his ribs broken shortly before his death, or perhaps even after he was hit with the gun or perhaps the hammer, to break his ribs. It seems unnecessary to strike a victim when he is already dead or dying but many killers go into what is known as 'overkill'.

Due to the fact his sister, who he had visited that day, and his wife and friends had not known of him having broken his ribs or having suffered any injury, it was obvious to detectives that he had suffered this further injury shortly before or immediately after his death and almost certainly at the hands of his killer. For a man to have broken his ribs and then been shot dead in two separate, unconnected incidents would stretch

the limits of possibility a little too far. The broken ribs were only revealed through the press following a second post-mortem examination. This caused the local papers to suggest that the first post-mortem had been botched but this was strenuously denied by Berrett: 'Actually we knew that from the start. It's obviously an important clue in our investigation.' He claimed the information was not revealed to the public at first because it was hoped it would be able to be used to identify the killer because only the police and murderer would have known about the broken ribs. The police decided to reveal the information perhaps because they were so confident that they would catch the person responsible that they did not feel they had to withhold facts from the public.

And indeed, the police revealed a large amount of information regarding their theories. The readers of the two local papers, the *Nottingham Evening Post* and the *Nottingham Journal*, will have sensed the frustrations and confusion of the detectives. All of the police theories were prominently featured, often on the front pages of the newspapers. Whilst the very high levels of confidence were initially evident in the articles written, the murderer would have had grounds to be confident too given that the reporters informed the public through their articles that the police believed a 12-bore gun to have been used, before changing their view and then changing their theory back again.

The second post-mortem was undertaken because the police had concerns about the number of pellets found in the wounds. Police determined the amount of pellets was far less than what you would expect from a 12-bore shotgun and this was a cause of great puzzlement. Detectives eventually announced the murder weapon must have been a far smaller type of gun. They did not believe the charge could have been home-made, with fewer pellets used. As a result the police began to focus their investigations on six men each of whom lived locally and had possession of a gun they believed was the type used in the killing. Their belief, changed, however, when they realised that there were in fact sufficient number of pellets found in and around the wounds and within the vehicle and therefore concluded a 12-bore shotgun had been used in the murder,

with one of the shots possibly having been fired from a distance, causing pellets to be lost. It was believed the first shot may have been fired from twenty-five yards away, with the murderer standing by a gate. This shot caused Samuel to lose control of the vehicle and come to a stop and then the gunman approached and fired the fatal shot in his face before making his escape with the best part of Samuel's takings for the day.

The broken ribs added a new dimension to the case as did the evidence of a witness who saw the vehicle after the murder had been committed. George Arthur Parke, of Windmill Cottages in Warsop was riding a bicycle along the stretch of road at 9.30pm. He told the local press: 'While I was cycling along I noticed a car beside the road with all its lights on. I was carrying a new acetylene lamp and flashed it into the car. I am prepared to swear that there was nobody in that car unless he was lying on the floor.' He was able to confirm that the vehicle was that driven by the victim and that it was in the same position when he saw it as it was found to be the following morning.

Was George Parke mistaken? It would seem so. The evidence available does not support any belief that Samuel was killed outside the vehicle and his body placed inside at a later point in time. There was no blood outside the vehicle or underneath the doors so it is indisputable that he was shot whilst in the driver's seat. Nonetheless Parke's account was information that made the police investigation more confusing.

Was Samuel the intended victim? It was always assumed that he was. According to a former Warsop resident, it was well known that Samuel would drive home at night with a large amount of money on him after he had finished his collections of payments for his groceries.

The weapon used in the crime was assumed to be a sporting gun which was not folding, the sort used by poachers and as the investigation progressed there was an increasing belief that a poacher was responsible for the murder, to the point that the police ruled out all other possibilities and focussed their resources solely on known poachers. If they had reason to believe, beyond all doubt, that a poacher was responsible then this may have been wise. However, the fact that Samuel's murder remains unsolved eight decades on suggests the police

may have made a terrible assumption that prevented them from catching the culprit because they were looking in the wrong direction. The county of Nottinghamshire was said to be 'plagued' by poachers who were usually in small gangs of three and often had access to a vehicle.

A poacher may not necessarily have been responsible. Whilst poachers are accomplished at hitting moving targets, and therefore would have been competent at shooting Samuel whilst driving, equally former soldiers and many farm workers experienced at shooting rabbits, birds and other 'pests' would have been able to carry out such a crime, and there were plenty of these types of people in rural Nottinghamshire twelve years after the First World War. Nonetheless, several poachers were targeted in the police investigation. Daddy Reynolds was the best known poacher according to a source of mine. He was questioned at length but eliminated. A farmer and his three brothers were also questioned and had their shotguns confiscated but there was no evidence suggesting their involvement in Samuel's death.

On Thursday 25th, two men were questioned. One of these claimed he had been tending to his fowls at around 9pm when he saw a beam of light coming from the road where Samuel met his end. The man heard two shots being fired and then the light went out. If the man's story was true, he did not think the occurrence was worthy of speaking to the police at the time of the incident. The police failed to find any information linking him to the crime other than he claimed to be in the area when it was committed.

The police quickly determined a motive of robbery. However, prior to reaching this firm conclusion there had been speculation among the public and the press to other theories. The first was that Samuel had committed suicide, a theory that was easily discounted on consideration that the weapon used was nowhere to be seen. Then there was the belief that Samuel had been giving a poacher a lift somewhere and during the journey the gun had accidentally discharged. Such a theory seemed implausible given two separate shots were fired, from different distances, but it probably helped sell newspapers and gave the local population extra gossip.

The victim never owned a gun and he had no links, as far as could be established, with any criminal activity or any association with criminals. He was not the type of man who had enemies as far as everyone who knew him was concerned.

One of Samuel's brothers, Mr WH Wilson of Chesterfield Road, Mansfield, told the press that he believed robbery must have been the motive. 'So far as I can judge it you can rule out any question of suicide. No one was fonder of life than my brother. He had no troubles that I know of and he had no more enemies than anyone else. I don't think there was any question of any debtor being pressed for money. The firm are not hard so far as money is concerned. I am puzzled that only £6 should have been found on him. I should have thought it would have been nearer £26. I have been the Clipstone round myself so I know what he would collect.'

Despite the account books suggesting he had collected only approximately £6, the police eventually became convinced that the killer stole at least £20 and there was the belief Samuel may have had as much as £22 taken from him.

The police were immediately confident that they would apprehend the individual responsible for the brutal murder. On day two of the investigation Chief Inspector Berrett told the press that whilst the killer would not be caught that day, they had made significant advances: 'We have narrowed the inquiry but there is no possibility of an arrest tonight.'

On Monday 29 September, the press reported that the police were once again very confident of a breakthrough very soon indeed and that they were certain the murderer was a local man who knew his victim's movements. The reason for their increased optimism was that the murder weapon had been found. The gun's owner was known to be a Warsop man and police brought him in for questioning though despite him having owned the murder weapon, they could obtain no evidence linking him to the crime associated with the gun. The police had also gained information of a new sighting of the killer shortly after the murder.

A stallholder on Mansfield market was walking through the market with a friend on the night of the murder when he was approached by a hawker. The hawker asked the two men

whether they would be interested in buying a gun, which he presented to them removing it from a bag before firing it in the air to demonstrate that it worked. The men were not interested and they walked away. The police were confident that this was the murder weapon and the short amount of time between the murder and the encounter on Mansfield market meant that the hawker was probably Samuel Wilson's killer.

A barn on a farm quarter of a mile from where Samuel was shot dead held clues that enabled the police to make major advances in their investigations. The barn had not been used by the farmer in a long time. It had not been used for storage of hay for a number of years but the farmer's sons had occasionally kept their guns in the building up until a few months prior to the tragedy. The farmer confirmed that no one, to his knowledge, had set foot in the barn for several months and nobody had the authority to do so. However, detectives were quickly able to establish that somebody had indeed been sleeping in the barn very recently and that they had left in a hurry. A well, very close to the barn, had its covering boards removed and hurriedly replaced. It is said that it was at the bottom of this well that the murder weapon was found, though the police never confirmed this.

And there was soon another potential clue. Two bloodstained bank notes had been passed by a woman in a Nottingham pub over the weekend of Saturday 27 and Sunday 28 September. There was the belief that a woman, perhaps this woman who was in possession of the banknotes, may have been shielding the killer and was too afraid to come forward. This led to the Scotland Yard detectives concentrating their energies on nearby Nottingham in the hope of identifying the woman and determining where and from whom the money had been obtained and to determine whether the notes were part of any money that could have been stolen from Samuel Fell Wilson. Meanwhile the local Nottinghamshire police continued to pursue leads in Warsop with the belief that the killer did live locally.

One week into the investigation, 300 people had been questioned and given statements. Suspects and witnesses were being questioned at a dentist's shop across from the police

DCI James Berrett, one of Scotland Yard's finest detectives. History By the Yard

station because Mansfield police station had insufficient facilities to enable questioning to take place there. Nosey members of the public were often seen peering into the windows of the police station and following detectives at any and every opportunity. Such was the public interest in the story that a school boy who helped sell the *Nottingham Evening Post* was called out of school early on the day of the discovery of the murder and sold three times as many newspapers as usual. On the Sunday night a man had been questioned for five hours before detectives conceded that they could gain nothing enabling them to show the man was the killer. They released him at 1.30am.

Despite a failure to uncover evidence leading them to a suspect, detectives told the public and press that they were simply 'marking time' until they got their man. They were optimistic, they said, that they would certainly capture the local poacher responsible for the heinous crime. And indeed they soon announced they were getting closer to solving the mystery.

By the beginning of October, the police went to the press with news that they had a prime suspect. They informed the public that a local man, well known to police was, in their opinion, the killer. Of this they had little doubt but no evidence. It was a theory based upon the fact that he was a poacher with a criminal record for poaching. Despite subjecting the suspect

to intense questioning they had not obtained information proving his guilt and they had insufficient evidence to make an arrest. The police revealed that the man owned a sports gun but no reference was made to whether he had access to the gun used in the murder, which the police were by that time in possession of. Desperate to link the unnamed man to the crime, they appealed for anyone who had information about the suspect's movements on the night of Samuel Fell Wilson's murder, to come forward. Their appeal did not achieve what they hoped it to, but how could it when the police never actually released their suspect's name?

On the night of Thursday 16 October, a suspect was interrogated at length without any useful information having been gleaned. With their hopes dashed detectives lost their optimism although they still believed they would bring the killer to justice. After taking part in a conference of top police officers in Nottinghamshire, Chief Inspector Berrett and Detective Sergeant Harris returned to London. They had

Letters sent to detectives claimed that a man had confessed to Samuel's murder.
Author's collection

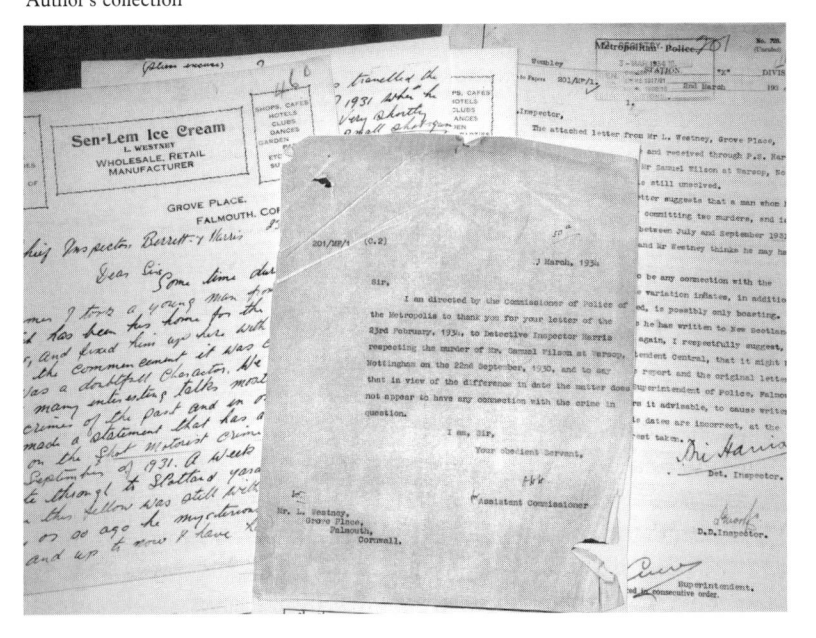

returned to the capital briefly once before during their Nottinghamshire case, but this time they gave no indication as to when, if ever, they would return. A portfolio of the evidence they had uncovered was sent to the Chief Commissioner of Scotland Yard in case he was able to offer any advice as to the mystery but a belief that the killer would be captured soon began to disappear and the case soon slipped out of the news.

Occasionally, over the next four years, the police would have a new lead that led nowhere and they would have to expose the bulging murder files to the elements once again. In March 1934 the now Detective Inspector Harris dismissed the contents of a letter received by the police, as someone with a 'fabrication' of a man's 'fertile mind' seemingly 'boasting' of having committed murders and armed hold-ups. The letter was written by a Mr L Westney who had employed a man who he suspected may have killed Samuel Fell Wilson. According to Westney, the unnamed man had confessed to killing two men after his discharge from the army and he was said to have carried a gun between July and September 1931. Westney's letter states that he and the man had many discussions about past crimes and during one of the discussions the man allegedly made a statement that has a 'direct bearing on the shot motorist crime at Warsop in September of 1931'. A few days after making what was considered to be a confession, the man 'mysteriously disappeared'. The man had apparently often expressed an ability to rob someone as they were driving along a stretch of road.

Harris did not see the lead to be worth following. He wrote: 'There would not appear to be any connection with the latter mentioned crime [the murder of Samuel], owing to the variation in dates, in addition the employee, whose name is not mentioned, is possibly only boasting.' Of course, the dates were wrong but could the unnamed man have been giving a veiled confession? Or, given that Westney had said the murder took place in September 1931, could the man or Westney himself been confused about the dates? The detective refused to speak to Westney and thought it of no value to try and locate the man. Was he boasting or had he indeed committed murders? Or were the contents of the letter in fact a fabrication of Westney's

A memorial to all those who have died in Warsop: Lest We Forget. The author

mind? As he was never spoken to, these are questions that could never be resolved.

The dismissal of Westney's letter was the last action carried out by those employed to find Samuel's murderer. The hunt was over and the police files once again were left to accumulate a thick layer of dust. This was in stark contrast to the situation little more than a week after the shooting. On 1 October, a police official told the *Nottingham Evening Post* that there was no doubt the killer would be swiftly brought to account: 'It is only a question of hours now before our week's investigations will be brought to a definite conclusion.' Nearly eighty years after the death of Samuel Fell Wilson there is indeed a definite conclusion: that his killer has got away with murder.

CHAPTER 5

George Harry Tyler: Clay Mills

1947

Despite having taken place more than sixty years ago, the death of George Harry Tyler is one that is still occasionally spoken of, and well remembered, by those living in a small village just outside Derbyshire. It was, as the inquest into his death determined, a 'most brutal and callous murder' but for all the talking, and despite a nationwide manhunt, the mysterious man responsible for the crime has never been identified.

George Tyler was a twenty-six-year-old taxi driver and it was whilst carrying out his job that he met his untimely end. His

The spot where George was shot in his taxi. The author

body was found in the back of his taxi cab at around 8.30am on Wednesday 30 April 1947. The vehicle was located on the main Derby Road, the A5112, near Clay Mills, Stretton, in Staffordshire. George had been shot dead.

Four bullets had been fired from within the taxi. One had been fired at the windscreen whilst the others had been fired at George, passing through his left lung, heart and head, where they remained lodged. There were further wounds inflicted after the man's death; a wound to the right eye, a small wound in the right eyebrow and a further wound in George's back. Death, it was found, was caused by shock and haemorrhage due to the passage of the bullets through the major internal organs. The gunman wanted to ensure his victim had no chance of survival.

The bullets recovered from the body were sufficient evidence for the police to conclude that the murder weapon was a .38

George Harry Tyler: an artist's impression. Vicki Schofield

calibre revolver of the sort provided to those in the armed services. Indeed, it would appear that George Harry Tyler was murdered by an officer of the Royal Air Force or, at the very least, a man who wanted to provide the impression he was in the RAF.

It did not take the police long to determine the identity of the victim, due to them tracing the ownership of the taxi. David Taylor, of 104 Bordesley Green, Birmingham, formally identified the victim as George Harry Tyler who lived at the same address. They had been business partners since both men left the RAF after the Second World War, having served together throughout the war, and had based their business in Birmingham having saved up enough money to buy two cabs. 'I can't understand why anyone should do such a thing. He had not an enemy in the world,' Taylor's father had told the *Burton Daily Mail* who devoted huge coverage to the case. After the death of George's parents, Taylor's family had come to regard George as one of their own.

Of course, such a phrase following the murder of a loved one, has become almost a cliché. Extensive enquiries, however, failed to identify anyone with a grudge that would have provided motive to murder the taxi driver.

Taylor last saw his partner at 10pm outside Birmingham's New Street railway station. George has been stood beside his taxi, waiting for a fare. It was at this location that George picked up his murderous customer at some point between 10pm and 10.30pm. A detailed description was offered to the police, who announced that the man they were hunting was: 'Aged 25 years, 5ft. 8in. in height, round face, with fresh complexion, but looked rather pale; clean shaven, dark hair, dark eyes; spoke with middle-class Midland accent; dressed in R.A.F. battledress and forage cap; seemed to be agitated when hiring a taxi.'

Detective Inspector F Tucker, one of the senior investigating officers, believed the airman stole from his victim and this was the reason for the crime: 'We believe that robbery was the motive behind the murder, for very little cash was found on the body, and it is believed that George had at least 30s when he left Birmingham,' the detective told the local press.

However, it seems unbelievable that the killer travelled to Birmingham, and from there got a taxi, solely to commit a murder motivated by robbery and then, after committing the robbery, travelled across three counties, as soon will be discussed, before travelling to Derby. Why would he have chosen to pay for a taxi journey from Birmingham to Derby (a forty-mile journey) when he would have only had to wait forty-five minutes for a direct train? It is quite conceivable that he was from the area and travelled to Birmingham by train, on his way home during a period of leave or he was on his way back to an RAF base to recommence service following a period of leave. Why though did he travel to Birmingham if his intended destination was Derby when he could have got a direct train from London to Derby or, as has just been stated, changed in Birmingham and reached his destination by rail? It seems implausible that he travelled to Birmingham in order to rob a taxi driver and no other reason. He could have robbed anyone, anywhere, so why did he get into George's cab?

I believe George Harry Tyler was deliberately targeted by his killer. This is a view shared at the time by some of George's relatives and it is a view shared by some of George's surviving family who I have spoken to during my research.

One relative informed me: 'I have no evidence that George was the intended victim, it may well be that he just happened to be in the wrong place at the wrong time although that goes against everything the family has ever thought... My grandmother and my mother both say that he was a bit of a 'so and so' and they firmly believe that it was someone from his past that he had crossed during his time in the airforce.'

According to his surviving relatives, George served at Bletchley Park, carrying out radar work. Could he have met his killer during his wartime service? Whilst there is no evidence to suggest the victim recognised his killer, equally there is no evidence to prove he did not know his killer.

It was, for a time, considered that a London gang had been responsible for the execution-style kill. However, this possibility was soon ruled out although it was accepted the killer had probably come from London, travelling by train to Birmingham shortly before getting his cab.

The reason behind the theory that a London gang could have been responsible, was that on the day of George's death, another murder had taken place in the West End of London.

At 2pm on the afternoon of 29 April, Charles Henry Jenkins (age twenty-three) who was known to police as the 'King of Borstal', Christopher James Geraghty (twenty-one) and Terence Peter Rolt (seventeen) robbed a jeweller's shop in Charlotte Street in London's West End. Wearing masks and carrying revolvers, they burst into the shop, jumped over the counter and attacked the director of the company, Alfred Stock, leaving him bleeding from a head wound. They demanded the manager of the shop, seventy-year-old Bertram Keates, to open the safe. Keates refused and threw a stool at the armed men. One of the robbers fired a shot at Keates but missed, at which point the men ran away but their getaway vehicle had been blocked in by a lorry. They ran down the street and shot a motorcyclist, Alec De Antiquis, who got in their way. He was shot in the head and soon died from his injury. They were quickly caught, charged, tried and convicted with Rolt, sentenced to imprisonment, being released in 1956, and with the other two men both having been hanged.

Understandably, the police had to consider a potential link between the two murders, both of which involved a gun and both of which were motivated by financial gain, but the police seemed satisfied that the crimes were not connected, especially after the London gang was caught and questioned, with Rolt having been particularly keen to inform the police of everyone involved in the attempted jewellery heist. The gang only consisted of three men and none of them had headed up north following the botched robbery.

Before leaving Birmingham, George and his passenger called at the Pearce Service Garage, on Great Charles Street, Birmingham. Mr HG Evans, who served the doomed man, said that the taxi's passenger looked like an Air Force man and he seemed 'dozy' – as if he had just woken up and looked around, wondering where he was – before seemingly going back to sleep.

From there, George's taxi headed along the main Burton to Derby road, in the direction of Derby where the airman had

asked to be taken, stopping at the village of Clay Mills just outside Burton on Trent, where the crime took place.

A resident remarked to the local paper, the *Burton Daily Mail*, that she had heard the sound of a shot around 11.30pm but her husband had told her it was only a 'car that had gone wrong'. Neighbours reported other disturbances around the same time; a car was heard to suddenly stop moving, followed by the noise of doors being repeatedly shut and another neighbour told police that his dog began barking at 11.20pm but he personally heard nothing.

There were no real causes, however, for people's suspicions to be roused despite the noises. Indeed, between the time of the murder, which was presumably between 11.20pm and 11.30pm, and the police arriving at the scene at around 10am the following morning, hundreds of cars had passed the taxi with no one noticing anything suspicious. The taxi's lights were on at 9am when William Kenneth Mitchell, a bread deliverer for the Burton Co-operative Society, opened the door and switched them off, but even he did not notice anything he felt to be suspicious. He failed to see the dead man's body slumped in the back of the vehicle.

The taxi was taken to Birmingham, with the body still in the back seat, for examination by Professor JM Webster of the West Midlands Forensic Science Laboratory. Examination of the vehicle revealed that George had been killed whilst at the wheel and his body then moved to the rear of the vehicle. It could be that the gunman intended to drive the taxi away but fled, having left the lights on.

Two schoolgirls provided the police with a valuable clue. Late in the Wednesday evening, June Stanbridge and Doreen Harrison, both aged thirteen, went out to look for wild flowers for a school competition. They walked along Rolleston Road towards a bridge over a brook, at a point where one of the fences was broken. Climbing through the fence, they walked down the bank towards the water. In the water they soon saw torn pieces of a page from a book of clothing coupons. Water barely flowed at this point along the brook and so it was clear that the page had been torn in close proximity to where it was found. The girls began looking for more, on the grass, in the

water, but none were visible. They wandered over the bridge and had more success; the torn remainder of the coupon book had been crammed into a gap in the wall of the bridge along with a torn identification card and an RAF Service book. The name George Harry Tyler was clearly visible and June's father instantly recognised the name when the girls returned later in the evening. Mr Stanbridge looked through his daily paper for details of the crime and immediately telephoned the police who carried out a search of the area. Nothing else relevant to the crime was uncovered during the search. The ID card and clothing coupon books were tested for fingerprints but none were found that could not be accounted for since the torn papers had been found.

Ponds in the Horninglow and Rolleston area were emptied, brooks and streams were dragged, hedgerows combed and a detailed search of the ground was made in the hope that the murder weapon would be found. Two rounds of ammunition were found on a grass verge on Rolleston Road, near

A large pond next to the crime scene which was dredged for clues without success. The author

Horninglow Cross, about half a mile from where George's clothing coupon book and identity card had been found, at a location where an airman had been seen kneeling early on the Wednesday morning. No attempt had been made to hide the ammunition; it had just been left there. An Albert Cheetham, a belt moulder from the British Tyre and Rubber Company, was approaching a cross roads on his way home from work when he saw the airman standing on the left hand side of the road before he quickly dashed across and bent down on one knee, leaving the ammunition. This sighting had taken place shortly after 6am. There was a pond in the general area from which the airman was seen running. The local fire brigade drained the pond but no evidence was forthcoming from it.

Rather impressively, by 2 May 1947 civilian and RAF police had interviewed more than one thousand servicemen, but they came no closer to identifying the culprit.

Unusually, the police were able to piece together quite a detailed account of the movements of the gunman following his crime, though questionable sightings were also reported to detectives, as is so often the case.

A farm labourer on a motorcycle, for example, was riding from Long Eaton through Alvaston, on the outskirts of Derby, when he picked up a hitchhiker who happened to be a serviceman wearing an RAF-type Macintosh. The man got off the bike at Shardlow, near Long Eaton. However, this sighting took place three days before the murder, on Saturday. The same labourer reported seeing a vehicle matching the description of the taxi outside the Corporation Gasworks on Wetmore Road, Shardlow, at 2.15am, a little under three hours after the murder. A man in a peaked cap allegedly was seen running back to the vehicle before driving off. Police did not believe the sightings were related to the crime. Nonetheless, police continued to hunt this individual and although his presence might appear to be suspicious he might have simply been a deserter from the RAF. Indeed, during their hunt for George's killer, detectives located at least fifty servicemen who were Absent Without Leave.

At some point between 2am and 3am, just hours after George was killed, an airman who was believed to be the

murderer, was seen walking along the main road towards Derby, by a number of lorry drivers. The important question to ask is, if this man was the killer, where was he from the time of the murder and the time of this sighting? The crime itself took place around 11.30pm and yet the Burton to Derby road is only approximately ten miles long. Could the killer have stayed around the crime scene for a while before embarking on his walk towards Derby? Or could the Sharlow sighting have been correct, with the airman having driven the taxi to Sharlow before returning to where the murder had occurred, having put George in that rear of the taxi in order to be able to drive? It seems unlikely but the fact remains that the gunman, for whatever reason, was in no hurry to make good his escape.

He was then seen, as described previously, at Rolleston shortly after 6am. A second witness saw him in the area, at 6.30am, walking along Rolleston Road towards Horninglow, which is closer to the centre of Burton-upon-Trent. He had evidently decided to turn round and return to Burton on Trent, taking a circuitous route, rather than continue walking for five

Wyggeston Road, where the murderer asked for directions. The author

Burton Railway Station, where George's killer waited calmly for a train to Derby.
The author

or six miles to Derby. No doubt the exposure to a large number of passing vehicles and their drivers had caused the murderer to have a heightened sense of fear of being captured.

By 6.55am he had reached a bus stop near Wyggeston Street, close to Burton town centre, where he asked a workman the way to Burton train station. At 7.30am he asked another local the way to the station. He finally arrived at the Burton train station at 7.40am and bought a ticket to Derby before going to the refreshments room at 7.45am where he stayed for half an hour, enjoying a cup of tea and the best part of two pieces of cake. He boarded a train to Derby at 8.20am.

Approximately twelve hours after the murder, a car belonging to a doctor on his honeymoon was stolen in Nottingham. Four hours later it was found abandoned in Markfield, near Leicester, thirty miles from Nottingham, with a suit having been taken from the vehicle. A man was seen leaving the vehicle and according to police the individual matched the description of the killer. If George's murderer did

indeed steal the car in Nottingham, and the police had no doubts that he did, then his movements are incredibly erratic; to travel presumably from London to Birmingham, shoot someone between Burton-upon-Trent and Derby, walk towards Derby, before turning back towards Burton only then to get a train to Derby and from there travel to Nottingham before stealing a car and abandoning it in Leicestershire. It is rather unusual and puzzling behaviour. Perhaps he intended to confuse those searching for him but in doing so he opened up many risks that could have led to his capture.

The fact the man spoke with a posh Midlands accent and the fact he travelled to small villages in Staffordshire and Leicestershire, but managed to find his way to main towns and cities, albeit with some assistance from locals, implies he had a vague knowledge of the geography of the Midlands region. However, his military training would have assisted him in his attempts to evade capture and may have influenced the seemingly erratic nature of his movements.

The variations of criminal behaviour are finite. With new technology crime can and does change but only to a point. There are only so many different types of crime that can be committed and it is often the case that a crime committed today may be similar in many aspects to an offence committed years or even decades previously. This is certainly the case in the murder of George Harry Tyler.

On 6 October 1944, Karl Hulten, a Swedish-born but American citizen who had deserted from the American Airforce whilst stationed in England, robbed a taxi driver in Hammersmith with his accomplice Elizabeth Jones. On a lonely stretch of road Hulten asked the driver to stop the vehicle, at which point the airman shot him in the head, stole his vehicle and spent the money the following day at a racetrack. Hulten was hanged for the murder in March 1945.

An even more eerily similar murder took place in 1920 involving Francis Percy Toplis, who is often referred to as the Monocled Mutineer for his speculated involvement in a mutiny in India (the Etaples Mutiny), but who was known by several aliases including Francis Edmunson, Percy Francis and William Wilson.

Toplis was born in Chesterfield in Derbyshire and even matched the description of George's killer. In 1920 Toplis was twenty-three years old, 5 foot 7 inches tall, with a fresh complexion, light brown hair with ginger moustache (though he was sometime clean shaven), blue eyes, medium build and two teeth missing from his top jaw and a false tooth on his bottom jaw.

Toplis had a criminal record including the offences of rape and fraud. He was, however, in the Royal Army Services Corp, which he joined in 1920. Previously, prior to spells in prison, he had served in the Royal Army Medical Corps during the First World War.

On 24 April 1920, Toplis went AWOL. Later that day he shot dead a taxi driver named Sidney George Spicer, on Thruxton Down near Andover. Toplis had been dressed in the uniform of an RAF officer. A manhunt was undertaken to find the killer and he was eventually shot dead in a gunfight while evading arrest, on 6 June 1920.

Obviously Toplis was not involved in the murder of George Harry Tyler, because he had been dead twenty-seven years but it can easily be argued that the similarities between the murders of the taxi drivers are too similar to be just a coincidence. Could it be that the man who killed George was trying to perform an almost identical murder to that committed in 1920 and the one similar to that committed in 1944? Could he have therefore been a copycat killer? It is a possibility worthy of consideration.

Despite a huge manhunt for the killer of George Harry Tyler, with Superintendent Lockley and his team often working until 3am in the morning, no credible suspects were identified. 'It is just a matter of waiting,' Lockley informed the *Burton Mail*, 'Scores of RAF personnel have already been interviewed but there is always the possibility that the man wanted for questioning was not in the RAF, but merely wearing the uniform. It may also be that he was recently discharged or he may still be serving. The hunt will go on until the case is brought to a satisfactory conclusion.'

Unfortunately the case was not brought to a satisfactory conclusion and the hunt for the murderer of George Harry Tyler continues. Murder files are supposedly never closed but

sixty-one years after George's death, Staffordshire Police confirmed to me, following Freedom of Information Act requests, that they lost all of the paperwork associated with the investigation into this shooting some years ago. When exactly these papers were lost is unknown but one thing is certain: even if George's killer is still alive, with no police records of this crime, short of him confessing, it is safe to say he has got away with murder.

CHAPTER 6

George Wilson: Sneinton

1963

The *Fox & Grapes* pub in the Sneinton part of Nottingham, next to the wholesale market, was known locally at the 'pretty windows pub' on account of its coloured glass windows and it was a popular drinking establishment. On Sunday 8 September 1963, it became known for far more than its windows, however, when its forty-three-year-old licensee, George Wilson, was brutally murdered.

George and his wife Betty had run the pub for more than a year, having left the *Walton Hotel* in Chesterfield in May 1962. The couple had become very popular, with regulars describing George as a cheerful and kind father of two young children.

Indeed, the hours leading up to George's tragic death had witnessed his customary humour and entertaining. Those drinking in the pub had enjoyed a sing-song until closing time

The Fox & Grapes *pub in 1963*. Reg Barker/www.picturethepast.org.uk

at 10.30pm and after the final customers left before 11pm the couple continued to entertain friends Anthony Smith, Arthur Ash and his wife. Mr and Mrs Ash were helping run the bar and Anthony Smith was a barman. The five friends were drinking in the lounge and after a few minutes they heard someone knocking on the side door of the pub. Betty Wilson went to answer the door but no one was around. She returned to the lounge and continued entertaining her friends.

After thirty minutes, Mr and Mrs Ash made their departure, followed by Anthony Smith who left in a taxi at 12.15am. George accompanied Smith to the taxi having brought his rough-haired mongrel Blackie outside to take the dog for a walk. George would habitually take his beloved pet for a fifteen minute stroll in the early hours of every morning before heading to bed.

What happened after Smith's taxi departed will never be known with certainty. All that is known is that within fifteen to twenty minutes George was dead. George had, at some point during the attack, dropped his keys indicating that he was about to unlock the door after having finished his walk, or he had just locked the door when the attack began. Mrs Wilson was alerted to the fact something was wrong when she heard Blackie barking outside and scratching the door. The time was shortly after 12.30am when she went down to investigate. Opening the door she was horrified to see her husband laying face down in a pool of blood. She ran to the next street and flagged down a car to ask for help. While the two occupants of the vehicle tried to help, Betty phoned for an ambulance but by the time it arrived George was dead.

The killer had thrust a knife in the landlord's body and head again and again. In total the publican was stabbed thirteen times with a two-edged dagger in what was a frenzied attack that would leave a community in fear and that has left a police force baffled ever since. The man's body was left slumped at the doorstep and was surrounded by pieces of slate. The slate fragments suggested to police officers that the assailant might have jumped from the low roof of an adjacent building in order to surprise the victim.

The police launched what was to become the largest manhunt in Nottingham's history at that time but the mystery and fear was to escalate when death threats were made to other licensees in the area.

On Monday 9 September, two more licensees had their lives threatened with 'the same treatment as George Wilson'. Fred Perry, aged thirty-seven, of the *Travellers' Rest* in Lenton, and his wife were put under police protection as a result. 'We are terrified. The threat was made by telephone,' Mrs Perry told the press.

Roughly two minutes after that telephone call, Albert Gilbert, fifty-two, of the *Barley Mow* public house, approximately a mile from the *Fox & Grapes*, was told over the telephone that he was next on the list. The Chief Constable for Nottingham, Thomas Moore, said that the police were treating the threats as very serious. Were the threats made by the man who killed George Wilson? Or were they the hoax calls of a person who wanted to increase the feeling of fear that was already present within the community? Even nine and a half years later a call was made to the then licensee of the *Fox & Grapes*, Frank Whitehead, to inform him: 'It's your turn next.'

It may no longer have pretty windows, but the former Fox & Grapes *is still the centre of one of Nottingham's highest profile unsolved murders.* The author

Despite their best efforts detectives were unable to identify the individual or individuals responsible for the harrowing telephone calls. We shall therefore never know whether George Wilson's killer struck out of hatred of that individual or whether the murderer had intended to commit a series of crimes. Though if his intention was to kill a number of licensees, why did he give them warning? Was it some sick individual trying to scare people or could it indeed have been the murderer who was seeking further gratification by discussing a crime he had committed? Had the killer become confident in his belief that he would evade justice that he felt he could talk without any fear of being caught?

The possibility that the individual or individuals who made the calls had responsibility for the murder at the *Fox & Grapes*, became an increasingly strong lead when it emerged that George Wilson himself had received a death threat two months before he was killed.

The police were unsure whether they were seeking a lone killer or at least two individuals. The belief that the killer did not act alone seemed plausible given that George was accompanied by a dog known to be aggressive, especially with strangers and there seems to have been little or no struggle between the victim and his attacker or attackers. Could it even be that George and Blackie knew his killer?

There were no witnesses to the crime. However, a witness came forward with a description of a man who detectives thought was of interest to their enquiries. The sighting was of a man, who they dubbed 'The Running Man' seen running along Longden Street, from the direction of Bath Street, at 12.50am. He was wearing a trilby hat and a raincoat and was holding what the witness described as looking like a chisel, which detectives thought might have been the long knife used in the murder. He was running so fast, and without great care, that he nearly got knocked down by the witness, who was driving a security van. The clothing worn by the running man was the entirety of the witness' description, however, which hardly gave the police very much to go on but it was certainly a lead which suggested the killer fled the immediate vicinity of the crime scene on foot.

Police were unable to determine a definite motive for the crime. George had two £5 notes in his pocket, which had not been taken, neither had his keys to the pub, rendering robbery an unlikely motive although there was a Scottish gang operating at the time which was involved in breaking into pubs in the city. Indeed one man informed detectives that the *Fox & Grapes* was on a list of pubs to be raided and that the raid was to take place on the Saturday night or early hours of the tragic Sunday morning. Extensive questioning of the members of the gang and their known associates, which amounted to approximately one hundred and fifty people, failed to uncover any evidence of the gang's involvement in the crime or any evidence that a raid on the *Fox & Grapes* had been planned. The men had strong alibis but detectives still had their doubts about the accounts given by the men and considered trying to bring charges against them. What had seemed to be a promising lead amounted to nothing, as did the rumour that George owed money to a loan shark.

So why was George Wilson killed? Could it have been an attempted robbery that went wrong? Or, because George seemingly had no known enemies and had only been living in the area for a little over a year, could it be that he was the victim of a mistaken identity?

It did not take long for Nottinghamshire police to realise that they were out of their depth. Whilst, in recent years, Nottingham has been dubbed as a city with significant levels of violent crime, detectives were certainly inexperienced with such violence in 1963. And so on Wednesday 11 September, Scotland Yard took over the investigation of the murder. Detective Superintendent Frederick Gerrard and Detective Sergeant Jack Norden arrived in Nottingham that night and set about intensifying the hunt for George Wilson's killer.

For a period of three months after the fatal stabbing up to 140 police officers worked up to eighteen hours a day in pursuit of the killer. It would prove to be an expensive investigation in terms of money and resources. Indeed, by 23 December 1963 the investigation had cost £16,800. Nottingham Watch Committee had asked the city's finance committee for £16,800 to pay for the cost of the inquiries. The majority of the costs were to fund overtime to Nottinghamshire, Derbyshire and Derby police forces who had lent Nottingham officers.

During the intense investigation a massive 60,000 people were spoken to, 10,200 homes and 4,000 businesses were visited and 3,000 statements were taken. Appeals for information were screened at local cinemas and loudspeaker vans patrolled the streets, urging anyone with information to come forward.

The contents of thousands of dustbins were searched in the first two days alone following the crime, in the hope that the murder weapon would be found.

A search of the area, including the scouring of roofs, wasteland and searching in drains, recovered twelve knives, one of which may have been the murder weapon thought Detective Superintendent Rex Fletcher, head of Nottingham CID, but his gut feeling was soon shown to be incorrect. Fletcher appealed for anyone to inform them if they knew of an individual suffering from any injuries specially a dog bite, in the belief that Blackie may have tried to defend his owner, although examination of Blackie's teeth indicated he had probably not bitten anyone. Local hospitals were visited to see if anyone had received treatment for such a wound. This possibility led nowhere.

The extensive search for the knife used to kill George Wilson seemed to many to be a painstaking task that would not be fruitful. It was only on the ninth day that two schoolboys proved the pessimists wrong.

The boys had been playing in a ditch along the Nottingham to Radcliffe-on-Trent road when they came across a knife in its sheaf. The knife had a double-edged steel blade, with a brass guard that was out of alignment and a brown leather handle with brass, red and black bands. The sheaf was brown leather with chrome rivets and a press stud fastener.

Tests confirmed that it was indeed the very same knife that had been used in George's murder. Traces of blood, of the same blood group as George's, were found. The tip of the blade had been slightly bent and as it was withdrawn from the victim's body it pulled out textile fibres which matched the clothing worn by George Wilson when he was killed. The blade was also the same size and shape as that of the murder weapon. Forensic examination failed to offer any clues to the ten-inch knife's owner, however, but old fashioned police enquiries brought a significant lead to their hunt for the man who discarded the knife.

An appeal for information in the Radcliffe area led to a new witness who claimed he had given a lift to a man on 11 September, three days after the murder. The motorist had picked up the man on the Nottingham to Radcliffe road, near the entrance to the Hoveringham Gravel Company, close to where the knife was found. The man was described as being 5' 8" tall, of thin build, pale complexion, receding auburn coloured hair which was brushed back and he wore glasses with no lower rim. The man was described as being around thirty years of age, although a *Nottingham Evening Post* employee drew a detailed sketch of the man, based upon the witness' description, depicting him as someone who looked quite significantly older than thirty, which cannot have helped the police in their hunt for the mystery man.

A further sighting was viewed as highly important, although the description was so vague that it did not provide much assistance to detectives. A taxi driver saw a man in a white coat banging on the door of the *Fox & Grapes* shortly before George was murdered. This was significant because this sighting was almost certainly of the knocking on the door to which Betty Wilson had gone to answer shortly after 11pm. Was this man connected to the attack? Appeals for him to come forward went unanswered.

Hotel guests in the Nottingham area were questioned and police appealed for a man and woman who had pulled up outside the *Fox & Grapes* at around 12.50am on the day of the murder to come forward. The man had asked the victim's wife, Betty, for directions to West Bridgford in Nottinghamshire.

Two months after the murder Betty Wilson received an anonymous note asking her to go to Derby bus station with £100 if she wanted to know who killed her husband. The meeting never took place because by the time it was sent, Mrs Wilson had left the *Fox & Grapes* and so she did not receive the note until after the date specified in the letter. Was it written by a crank who wanted to add to the suffering of the grieving widow?

On Sunday 15 September, detectives released a twenty-five-year-old Chesterfield man who had been 'helping the police in their enquiries'. There was no evidence to suggest he was George's killer. 'He is now free to go where he pleases,'

Superintendent Fletcher told the press. This Chesterfield man may have been Michael Copeland, who lived in Birdholme, Chesterfield at the time.

Copeland was eventually convicted of the Bubble Car Murder in Chesterfield along with two other murders; one in Chesterfield and one in Germany where he had served in the Army. By 1963, Copeland was the prime suspect in the three murders and detectives in Nottingham had considered a possible link between the Bubble Car Murder of June 1960 and the death of George Wilson. Indeed, Copeland's *modus operandi* was inflicting multiple stab wounds on his victims. However, despite Copeland being a highly disturbed individual, indeed a self-confessed psychopath, a motive for killing George Wilson was elusive, although George had been licensee of the *Walton Hotel* in Chesterfield, which was on the street on which Copeland lived at the time.

Copeland's victims in Chesterfield had been murdered because they were homosexual and it appears that Copeland was a closet homosexual who was ashamed of what he was and disliked those like himself. His victim in Germany, a young man killed as his girlfriend watched on, was murdered because Copeland had witnessed the pair having sex like he had seen his mother doing many times before. Police had to consider the possibility that the crimes were connected, and no doubt they did so partly in order to further their harassment on Copeland who was certainly being subjected to frequent covert and even overt surveillance between 1962 and 1965, but they eventually determined that the Bubble Car killer did not murder George Wilson.

If it was, as it seems likely, Copeland who was questioned by detectives, he was not the only known murderer to be questioned. Myra Hindley and Ian Brady were known to have visited Nottingham around the time of the murder and they found themselves briefly considered suspects. Detectives looked for links between other murders in the region. According to media reports at the time, they found no such murders.

In April 1964, detectives were led to a man in Grantham who bore a resemblance to the identikit picture of the man picked up near the gravel works. He was questioned for three days, and his garden dug up, but was eliminated.

A Nottingham killer named Frank Henry Wardle became a key suspect in the murder following his conviction for manslaughter on the grounds of diminished responsibility. Wardle had stabbed and beaten Arthur Fox, an elderly man with whom he lived at Baron Street, Nottingham, on 8 March 1965, at their home. Wardle confessed to the crime almost immediately upon carrying out the horrific attack. An expert later concluded that the killer had 'no signs or symptoms of mental illness' and that he was 'sane' but that he had an 'abnormality of the mind which limits his ability to act with foresight and which results in impulsive behaviour'.

Wardle had killed Arthur Fox because Fox had been 'moaning', according to his confession. Wardle had no previous convictions for violent offences, although he had eleven previous convictions including larceny and breaking into shops. He had been released from prison in May 1963 at which point he resumed working as a window cleaner. Upon killing Fox he had almost immediately telephoned the police.

Police files show suspect Frank Wardle confessed to killing another man in Nottingham. Author's collection

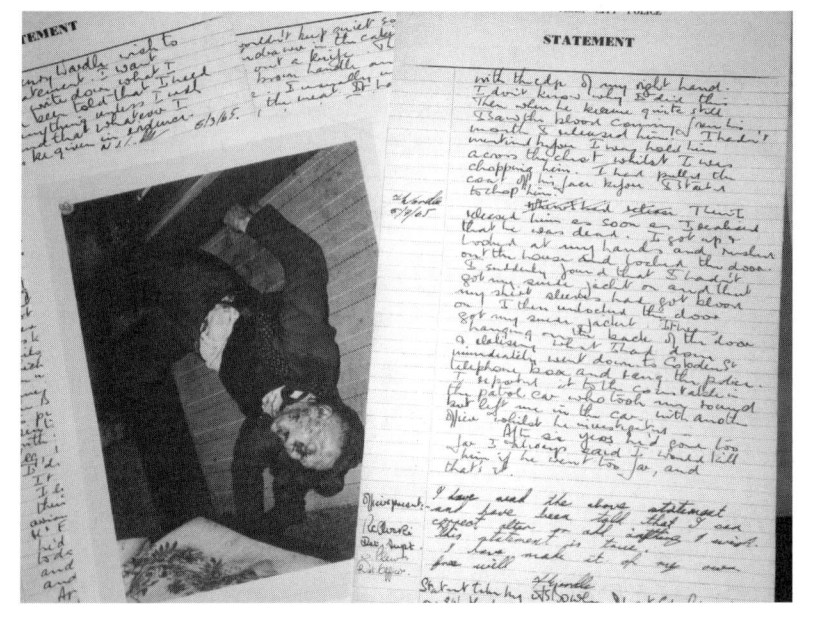

Detectives compiled a report for the Director of Public Prosecutions but they were told they had insufficient evidence to charge Wardle with the murder of George Wilson. Despite further enquiries they failed to find further information linking the convict to the Pretty Windows murder.

In December 1965, two detectives visited Dartmoor Prison to interview a prisoner there who they believed could have been responsible for the murder outside the *Fox & Grapes*. The interview was confirmed by Rex Fletcher, who had by this time been promoted to Assistant Chief Constable of Nottingham, who said 'we are making further inquiries'.

Their 'further inquiries' led to the man being eliminated from the investigation. It later transpired that he had confessed to the crime on no less than three separate occasions; his third being an eight page document detailing the crime written whilst he was serving a sentence for manslaughter. When the two detectives interviewed him the initial doubts they had had were confirmed. The prisoner had already failed to provide information about where he had hidden the murder weapon and when the distinctive knife was taken to him, along with seven others, the convict failed to identify the weapon he claimed he had used to kill the publican. His account of the incidents that led to George Wilson's death contained other questionable points.

In fact five men made confessions during the murder hunt, but none of them were deemed genuine. Nearly half a century on from George Wilson's murder, detectives who investigated the crime believe they know the identity of the murderer but they were always unable to find sufficient evidence. For years after the murder new information was being provided to police officers on an almost weekly basis, which is unique in criminal investigations. With forensic techniques having developed in recent years, there is always the hope that a breakthrough could still be made even after all these years and someone somewhere may have information that could help solve one of Nottingham's longest running murder mysteries.

CHAPTER 7

Mavis Hudson: Chesterfield

1966

The festive period should be one of goodwill, happiness and fun and it was with these thoughts in mind that two young boys searched derelict buildings near their homes at around 3pm on 27 December 1966. They were looking for materials to construct a play hut in order to make the most of their school holiday. Any festive cheer they had experienced was soon to disappear, however, when they approached the door to an outbuilding.

The boys caught sight of a black handbag, which was leaning against the door. Entering the small, filthy derelict building, something almost immediately caught their eyes. The boys were taken aback by the gruesome sighting of a semi-naked teenage girl laying on an old cement sack, surrounded by cardboard boxes and radio parts. She was wearing only black fishnet stockings. The boys did not have to go close to realise she was dead and they rushed up the road to one of their homes to raise the alarm. One of the boy's fathers visited the scene to make sure his son's story was truthful, before making the telephone call to the police.

Irene Hudson's Christmas cheer was ended and her life was shattered as she heard the traumatic news that her fifteen-year-old daughter had been murdered.

Mavis Hudson was a challenging child. She had been unruly and too difficult to look after for her widowed mother and so she had been sent to live in a children's home. Although, at the time of her death, Mavis had lived in a home in Bolsover, she had previously lived at a home on the bottom of Cobden Road on the outskirts of Chesterfield town centre, where she was well known by the children who lived in the area and disliked by many of them because of her lifestyle, which was beyond her

years and against the traditional views of the families in the area, many of who's children attended the strict Roman Catholic school on Cobden Road.

Mavis might have only been fifteen but she was far from being an innocent child. She smoked and regularly went out drinking. She also had many boyfriends, much older than her, who she would spend nights with. Often she would be picked up by a different man each night.

She had recently begun a hairdressing course at the local college, and had an ambition to eventually own a salon, but this did not give her sufficient stability as far as her mother was concerned.

Doctor Usher, who later carried out the post-mortem examination on Mavis Hudson's body, found that the deceased had died from asphyxiation caused by pressure on the neck and/or suffocation. He estimated she had been killed at some point between 10pm on 26 December and 1am the following morning.

The scene of the crime in the 1970s. Chesterfield Photographic Society/www.picturethe past.org.uk

Spa Lane today. The author

The scene of the crime was a derelict outbuilding belonging to what had once been the Scarsdale Brewery on Spa Lane in Chesterfield. The Scarsdale Brewery buildings had been closed in 1960 and the following year all but the vaults and offices had been demolished, with the remaining buildings being left derelict.

Spa Lane is located just off St Mary's Gate, only a short distance from Chesterfield's famous crooked spire church, but despite being within the town centre, its location allows an easy escape route with a minimal chance of being seen. The killer could have fled in the direction of Birdholme, prior to the bypass being built, but on a cold, dark night the killer could have slipped away or driven away without anyone's suspicions being aroused. A few houses were located on the Lane but in the early hours of the morning the chances of being seen were remote. The killer must have known that.

When trying to reconstruct Mavis' movements in the hours leading up to her death, the police were confronted with conflicting accounts, which made the investigation far more

complex and probably contributed to the killer evading justice. It is difficult to determine who the last person to see Mavis before she met the person who ended her life, was. This is because the locations of sightings of Mavis contradict one another.

Much of the evening of Mavis' death had been spent with her mother, at her home on Augustine's Avenue, Chesterfield. After their evening meal they both went to the *Sun Inn*, on West Bars, in the town centre, arriving at around 7.25pm. Mavis was wearing a light blue coat, black pinafore dress over a black polo-neck sweater, black fishnet stockings and black patent leather shoes. She was a slim girl, with blue-green eyes and had black hair that was cut short with a 'mod' fringe parted in her forehead. She was carrying her new black handbag and a box of Cadbury's Contrast chocolates. Irene Hudson worked at the pub, as a bar maid, and her daughter stayed with her until just before 8pm. Mavis had told her mother that she needed to be at the children's home by 9pm. Irene Hudson would later change her story, at her daughter's inquest, testifying that

The Sun Inn. The author

The streets where Mavis is said to have been. Mr RM Wilsher (photographer)/www.picture thepast.org.uk

Mavis had not said anything regarding needing to be back at the home by 9pm.

However, in order to get back to Chesterfield from Bolsover, Mavis would have needed to catch the Number 28 bus at 7.57pm, at a cost of one shilling and threepence, and arrived at Bolsover Market at approximately 8.20pm. That night buses from Chesterfield to the nearby town left at three minutes to the hour up until 10.57pm. It would seem that Mavis accidentally missed her bus or deliberately did so having made alternate plans.

A girl who lived in Newbold, who was an acquaintance of Mavis, was certain that she saw the victim at 9pm walking alone along Lordsmill Street in the direction of Vicar Lane. Two separate sightings placed Mavis at the *Queen's Head Hotel* on Knifesmithgate. The witnesses, who knew the victim, claimed they had seen her at 9:45pm and 10:30pm. At 9.45pm she had been eating a meal with a girl according to a member of the bar staff. The other witness, a teenage boy, said he saw Mavis

The former Queen's Head. The author

at 10.30, leaning up against a juke box in the hotel's bar. However, these sightings were called into question when other witnesses came forward to say that Mavis was in Sheffield at those times. Some of the sightings had to be wrong.

A witness provided a statement saying that Mavis had been on board a bus travelling from Chesterfield to Sheffield at 8.45. The conductress later said that she too had seen Mavis on the bus at 8.30 and, importantly, she was with a group of youths. Whether Mavis was indeed travelling with these youths or whether she was simply being her flirty, friendly self during the journey, is not known but these individuals, none of whom were ever traced, could have provided vital information because they could have known how Mavis intended to spend her final few hours, if indeed it was Mavis who was seen. It is probable Mavis was intending to meet people in Sheffield, if she was not intending to spend time with those with whom she was seen

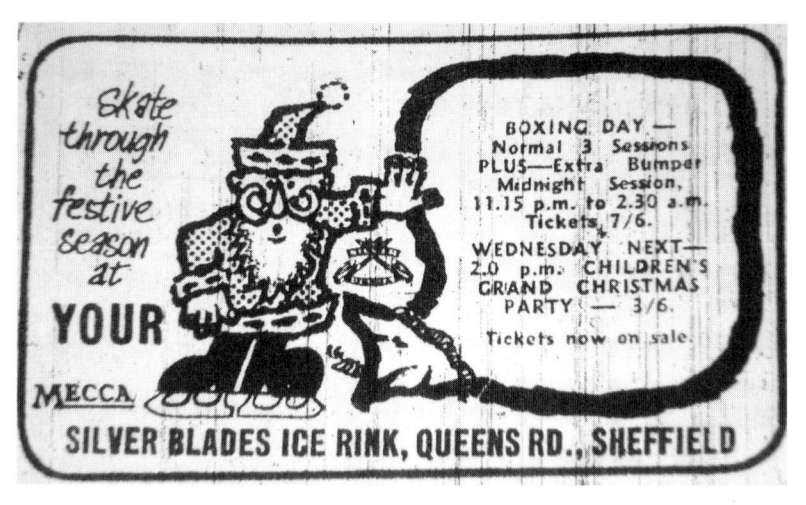

An advertisement for entertainment at the Silver Blades Ice Rink on the night of Mavis Hudson's death. Skate Central

The former Silver Blades Ice Rink where Mavis is said to have spent part of her final hours alive. The author

on the bus. It seems unlikely she would travel to Sheffield, and lie to her mother, if simply to spend time on her own, though of course such a scenario could never be ruled out.

A number of witnesses reported sightings of Mavis at the Silver Blades Ice Rink on Queen's Street in Sheffield at 10.45pm. The ice rink, located a few minutes walk from the city centre, had a number of sessions that day: 7:15pm to 10.45pm, with an admission price of 5/-, with 'Blaises' providing entertainment on stage and various 'skating exhibitions' taking place. Then later an 'Extra Bumper Midnight Session' from either 11pm or 11:15pm (two different times were printed in advertisements in Sheffield newspapers) to 2:30am on the morning of 27 December where for 7/6d skaters could watch a 'cabaret on ice' and enjoy music from the J Jones Jamboree Band.

The sightings of Mavis in Sheffield may not have been correct. The witnesses concerned did not know the victim. They had never seen her before and their identification was on the basis of a photograph of the victim which showed a police shorthand typist of Mavis' height and build, wearing identical clothing to that worn by the dead girl on the tragic night, with Mavis' head superimposed upon it to provide as best an impression of what the girl looked like on the night of her death.

If Mavis was indeed in Sheffield then she cannot possibly have been in the *Queen's Head Hotel* at the times witnesses claimed she was. It is possible she could have been seen on Lordsmill Street, but not at 9pm. Could the witness have been slightly wrong in her timing? Mavis was walking in a direction where there were bus stops that were on the route to Sheffield. Or were the Sheffield witnesses entirely mistaken? If Mavis was seen in the *Queen's Head Hotel* at 9.45 and 10.30pm she could not have been in Sheffield. So where did Mavis spend the evening and where did she meet her killer?

On Boxing Day 1966, a Sunday service was run for the city's buses, with the last bus from Sheffield to Chesterfield departing at 11pm. The previous bus left at 10.30pm and therefore, if the sighting of Mavis at 10.45pm is accurate she must have caught the last bus to Chesterfield or found some other means of travel.

If Mavis was in Sheffield that night and she caught the last bus from the steel city back to Chesterfield then she would have arrived in the town at around 11:50pm. If, however, she was not quick enough to reach the bus stop in time then she must have travelled by alternate means, perhaps with her killer, but if she was in Chesterfield all night at which point did she meet the person responsible for her death? Could it have been in the *Queen's Head Hotel*? Irrespective of whether or not Mavis travelled to Sheffield, there are no sightings of her between 8pm and 8.30pm, or 8pm to 9pm if she stayed in Chesterfield. Where was she during this time?

With Mavis conceivably having been in Sheffield so soon before her death the police may have been wrong to focus their attention predominantly upon Chesterfield in their high profile local appeals for information. The fact is she could, quite conceivably, have met her murderer in the South Yorkshire city.

There can be no doubt about the police's commitment to bring the killer to justice. Posters were put up on buses and in pubs, clubs, cafés, cinemas and other public buildings in Chesterfield to try and gain vital clues as to Mavis' movements before her death and to try and identify the person responsible. On New Year's Eve police officers were present at all twelve dances that took place in Chesterfield town centre because they believed it was likely anyone celebrating the New Year would have probably been in the town centre at around the time Mavis died and therefore they could be potential witnesses. At three cinemas in the town, a photograph of Mavis was shown on the big screen, along with an appeal for new witnesses to come forward. Slides of police appeals for information, featuring the edited photograph of Mavis Hudson, were shown whilst cinemagoers at the ABC watched Elvis Presley in *California Holiday* or *Hercules, Samson and Ulysses* and the Chesterfield Odeon screened Hayley Mills and Maurice Chevalier in *In Search of the Castaways* and *Dr Syn, Alias the Scarecrow*. And hundreds of people were questioned in bingo halls, dances, pubs and clubs in the days and weeks following the murder.

Plainclothes officers attended Mavis' funeral at St Augustine's church and burial at Boythorpe cemetery on

Tuesday 3 January 1967 in order to hunt out any strangers or anyone whose behaviour or expressions appeared to be suspicious. It was believed her killer might wish to attend in order to gain a higher level of pleasure from his crime, that he could have felt remorse for what he had done or that the murderer might have been someone close to Mavis who would be expected to attend and who may give some clue, by their behaviour whilst present. No such clues were obtained as the victim's friends and relatives gathered to pay their last respects.

The death of Mavis Hudson is unusual in that although the jury at the inquest into her death, which concluded in March 1967, ruled a verdict of 'death caused by person or persons unknown', it is more likely the case that the person who killed her intended to do exactly that. It seems the jury may have believed that the killer could have put pressure on the victim's neck, perhaps during some sex game, without meaning to end her life and that death was therefore an accident. The police do not believe this to be the case they are convinced it was murder. And the coroner at the inquest had difficulty accepting the jury's decision, asking them specifically whether they would like the word 'murder' inserted into their verdict after they had delivered it. They declined.

What was the motive for the crime? It was seemingly not robbery, for her handbag contained six shillings and tenpence and nothing seemed to have been taken from it. There was no evidence that she had had sex, although the girl's knickers were found beside her body and she was almost naked indicating some sexual motive. In its records, the Home Office has labelled the crime as one of 'unsolved murder committed during a sexual assault'. Strangulation and asphyxiation are usually, though by no means always, associated with a sexual motive because they require prolonged physical contact with the victim.

Following a death where foul play is suspected rumours will often spread throughout the area, growing ever more sensational with the passing of time. One such rumour was that Mavis engaged in prostitution. It must be stressed that there was no evidence to substantiate such a claim. However, this was a story that people believed before her death and so it could

be of significance and relevance. Even some children in the town knew Mavis' reputation, and believed it, whether it was true or not. The rumour was based upon Mavis' perceived loose ways in a period where many of the older generations in particular were conservative in their outlook. Mavis tended to be seen with different men each night, and was known to have many male friends with whom she would spend the night, which fuelled speculation even if it was erroneous. Could it be that someone who knew the girl's reputation made an unsolicited advance and refused to take no for an answer? It is quite conceivable that Mavis' reputation was the reason why she was murdered,

There were no indications that Mavis had struggled with her killer. There were no bruises other than those on her throat and there were no cuts or any other form of defence injuries. No one who lived in Spa Lane or the surrounding area reported hearing screams or anything of suspicion. Therefore for Mavis to have entered the outbuilding she must have done so of her own free will or she reluctantly cooperated with the person who ended her life.

The location of her murder is revealing. Spa Lane was an area frequented by 'courting couples'; people who were actually couples, people having affairs but also, occasionally, prostitutes and their clients. Forty years ago the car parks were not as well illuminated as at present and because the brewery was out of use and derelict, there were fewer people in the area than is the case now that the road is home to a popular bar.

No witnesses came forward to say they had seen anyone acting in a suspicious manner in or around Spa Lane around the period of time in which the murder took place. A car was seen, however, in the car park at the bottom of Spa Lane at 1am. Inside the car were a 'courting couple'. Police appealed for the couple to come forward but they never did. Did they see Mavis or her killer? Could the couple have even been Mavis and her murderer? Or were they just further evidence for the once unsavoury nature of the area in which Mavis Hudson's life was ended?

In the days following the discovery of Mavis' body a policeman was seen to be in a distressed state in a Chesterfield

pub. Unable to contain information about the case he confided in a small number of people a shocking belief over what the police allegedly believed happened to the dead girl. It was not a simple case of murder, he said. Instead the victim had been undergoing an illegal abortion that had gone wrong, it was claimed. Abortions had been illegal in England until 1967. Despite the provenance of this story there is no available evidence to substantiate such a shocking claim. Was he mistaken or was he acting with misconduct? Or was Mavis pregnant and perhaps killed by the father of the child? It is easy to speculate but it is a fact that the man who made the startling revelation was a police officer working on the case.

The police had no reason to believe that Mavis was definitely killed by a man, although it has been presumed that she lost her life at the hands of a male because of the perceived sexual motivation behind the crime. Indeed a sixteen-year-old girl, by the name of Susan Morley, was a suspect in the investigation. One of the witnesses who saw Mavis Hudson at the *Queen's Head Hotel*, informed investigating officers that Mavis was in the company of a girl who was believed to have been Morley. Morley was a fifteen-year-old Chesterfield girl at the time and was known to have run away from home. However, it was later determined, 'without any shadow of doubt' according to the police, that it was not Susan Morley who was sighted with the deceased because Susan had definitely been in Birmingham that night. Who was that girl? Did she play any role in Mavis' death or could she have simply been an innocent witness but an important witness who was one of the last people, if not the last person, to see the dead girl before she met her killer? Though, of course, Mavis may not have been there at all that evening.

The police did believe it was most probably a man who was responsible for the crime. They circulated an identikit picture of a man seen outside the *Sun Inn* around the time that the victim was there with her mother. It was stressed that the man was only a potential witness, but he was never traced.

Detectives did treat one man who was close to Mavis as a suspect in their investigation. A local man, who I shall call Bill, was repeatedly questioned in connection with the crime,

although he was never arrested or charged. Indeed he has argued the police tried to bully him into a confession during periods of intense questioning. A man with learning difficulties, Bill was a relative of the victim and, some of those who knew him have argued, an easy, vulnerable target. Someone who knew him quite well informed me that Bill was 'slow' but 'very gentle and would not have the brains to kill Mavis and get away with it, especially with the pressure the police put on him. They really interrogated him. It was like they were trying to make him confess whether he did it or not.' Bill never did confess, despite the best efforts of the police, and he never provided any incriminating evidence. All the evidence suggested he was totally uninvolved in his relative's tragic death.

So who did kill Mavis Hudson and why? Did he intend to cut short the fifteen-year-old's life or were the inquest jury right to believe death was caused inadvertently despite the strongly held beliefs of the police? Whatever the answer, more than four decades on, the person who killed Mavis Hudson has- so far- escaped the long arm of the law.

CHAPTER 8

Annie Walker: Heather

1969

A nnie Walker lived alone in Ivy Cottage, on Swepstone Road in the village of Heather, north-west Leicestershire, six miles from the Derbyshire/ Leicestershire border and eleven miles south or Derby. The reserved seventy-four year old was a popular member of the community, having been a former landlady of the *Queens Head* pub in the village for many years. She and her husband had owned businesses throughout their marriage and they had become reasonably wealthy as a consequence. Albert Walker had died several years earlier and Annie had

Swepstone Road, where Annie Walker was murdered in her own home. The author

The Queen's Head *in Heather, once run by Annie Walker and where the murder is still frequently discussed.* The author

continued to live in the red brick cottage they had shared, ever since.

It is said of most victims of murder that they had not an enemy in the world. This was certainly said of Annie Walker but somebody decided to inflict an act of evil violence upon her in April 1969.

On 2 April, the police had been called to Ivy Cottage as a result of concerns from a Mrs Atkins, a close friend who lived across the road. The pensioner had not been seen that morning and her bedroom curtains had not been drawn. This was

noticed at 7am and it was considered unusual for her to be awake at this time and so there were worries that she had not been to bed that night and that she may have been ill. Annie was a woman of habit who performed the same activities on a daily basis. Annie's neighbour would, at the pensioner's request, look each morning to see whether her curtains were drawn. Concerns were escalated when, later, Mrs Atkins saw smoke billowing out of the bedroom window.

Mrs Atkins ran out of her house and banged on Annie's door and shouted for the woman to answer but received no response. Scared and extremely worried, Mrs Atkins stopped a passing vehicle and got the driver to take her to Swepstone, where Annie's daughter, Maggie Forrester, lived. Mrs Atkins and Mrs Forrester quickly returned to Ivy Cottage and Mrs Atkins then ran to the local shop to call the fire brigade.

A police motorcyclist arrived on the scene first and forced his way into the building, through the back door, joined by two of the neighbours; farmer Tony Draycott and local coal merchant George Beresford who had been in the local shop when Mrs Atkins arrived. It did not take them long to see that the worst fears had been warranted. There had been a feeling of hope when Tony Draycott had climbed a ladder and got into the bedroom. He was able to establish that nobody was in the bed, which was on fire. Indeed it did not appear that anyone was in the bedroom at all. A fire engine arrived shortly after the men began their search of the building.

A scene of horror greeted the three men upon their entrance; Annie was found lying on the floor of the living room in her nightdress. It was clear that she was dead and had been for some time. She had been battered repeatedly around the head and lay in a pool of blood although at first it was not clear whether foul play had occurred or whether she had died as a result of a fall. A post-mortem would later determine that Annie was indeed murdered and the weapon used was a blunt instrument. It was found that the fatal blow had been inflicted while the victim was laying on the ground, presumably having already been struck a number of times.

The police officer called for assistance and soon seven police cars, a fire engine and an ambulance were on the scene.

Even the churchyard was searched for clues, to no avail. The author

The Coronation Street Murder, as it became known because of a character called Annie Walker who ran the *Rovers Return* in the soap opera (the victim had been a former landlady of a pub), began in earnest and was led by Detective Chief Superintendent Basil Saunders, head of the Leicester and Rutland CID. The village school became the temporary police headquarters. Sniffer dogs and every plain clothes police officer in Leicestershire and Rutland forces began searching for the weapon and Annie's missing handbag in the immediate vicinity of the crime scene but also in the fields and hedgerows in the village. A hedgerow across the road from the crime scene was hacked down in the hope the killer may have disposed of the weapon immediately after leaving the pensioner's cottage, but to no avail. The churchyard was not searched, however, until after Easter in order to respect the wishes of the many religious members of the community. Later, police frogmen searched ponds, reservoirs, streams and rivers in the hope of finding the weapon and bag, but their efforts were not rewarded with success.

One week after Annie's brutal murder, the police search had failed to locate the instrument of death and the missing handbag which had contained the huge sum of money, so they appealed to every man, woman and child living within a five mile radius of the crime scene to spend two hours to search every garden, field, allotment, roadside ditch and hedgerow. It was never found.

Detectives were able to establish a partial sequence of events preceding the violent crime. The cause of the fire in the bedroom was an electric blanket which had become overheated. Annie Walker was found in the living room in her nightclothes and the television and a table lamp were both switched on. It therefore seemed most plausible that she had switched the electric blanket on in order for it to warm up the bed before returning downstairs and shortly after her attacker struck, hitting her repeatedly and knocking her to the ground before striking the fatal blow. It was therefore deduced that the murder took place on the night before the body was discovered. The post mortem examination supported this theory.

The bedclothes in the bedroom had been disturbed, and were heaped up, and the police believed this was caused by the murderer searching through the house, moving the bedding and ultimately causing the fire that alerted the neighbours to the crime.

There was no evidence of forced entry into the cottage and police believed this indicated that the culprit had been known to the victim, or that Annie had answered the door and been overpowered. There is another alternative, of course; the killer could simply have opened the door and walked in, if Annie had still been up watching television in her lounge she might not necessarily have locked her door.

The motive was quickly established. Just hours before her death Annie had withdrawn £1000 (the equivalent of £15,000 in today's money) in £5 notes, from her bank account, having travelled to nearby Coalville to make the withdrawal. The police found her passbook showing the withdrawal had been made but it took several hours of meticulous searches of the cottage to determine the money had been stolen.

Coalville, where Annie's killer found his prey. The author

The reason for this substantial withdrawal was that she sought to reinvest her money although the withdrawal in £5 denominations, rather than obtaining a banker's draft, in my mind seriously questions such a theory. It was quickly established that the money had been removed from the bank account and it was discovered that all of the cash was missing from the pensioner's home. Annie was not facing financial problems, owing money to a loanshark or other such unscrupulous individual. Door to door enquiries and speaking to her relative failed to provide any evidence that Annie was in the habit of lending substantial amounts of money to anyone. She was not being blackmailed. This would seem to be a case of simple robbery and greed that turned to murder.

It is presumed the killer saw the victim withdrawing her money, or at least came to be aware that she had withdrawn the money, and followed her home or that he travelled to Heather at a later time, which seems most likely. Annie was killed in the evening or early night but she returned from Coalville by catching the 12.05pm bus meaning there was

several hours between the withdrawal and the killer entering her home. On the other hand though, if the murderer was not local and he did not follow Annie home, how did he know where she lived? None of the villagers were asked for any information about the victim before her murder. Perhaps the killer did follow Annie and then returned later that night if indeed he had been in Coalville earlier that day to witness the money being withdrawn. This seems the most likely explanation, the alternative, that the killer happened to burgle the house and got lucky by finding such a large sum of money, seems too much of a coincidence. None of the money was ever traced.

The police tried to locate anyone who Annie may have spoken to whilst in Coalville or on her return journey. A man she had sat with on the bus, and with whom she had engaged in conversation, became the focus of the investigation. He was described as wearing a blue anorak and a red fisherman knit jumper with a V neck. He had alighted the bus in Heather. However, the man was eventually traced, investigated and eliminated from police enquiries. He was unable to provide any information that assisted the police with their investigation.

Approximately 800 people were questioned during the course of door to door enquiries. Every man, woman and child (except young children) were deemed to be potential suspects and were questioned as such.

No one saw anyone acting suspiciously at or around Annie's cottage at the time of the murder or indeed in the hours or even days leading up to it. Indeed there was no one seen in the village acting in a manner conceived to be suspicious, at all. Bus drivers were questioned to see whether they could shed any light on the case, such as people who caught the same bus as Annie and perhaps showed unusual interest in her, or anyone who may have been seen following the victim. No information of significance was obtained from this source.

Three men were questioned by detectives during the course of their investigation. The main suspect was the third to be questioned at Coalville police station, being interviewed by Detective Chief Superintendent Saunders from the night of Wednesday 9 April through to the following evening. The two

Coalville police station, the headquarters for the investigation. The author

other men had both been questioned at length and were released on Wednesday pending further enquiries.

On Thursday 10 April, the police spoke of the good response they had received but emphasised the need for far more information. A police spokesman said: 'We are continuing to work hard and carefully. The public response to newspaper appeals has been first class and we are most grateful. But we still want to hear from anyone who has even the slightest crumb of information.'

Despite the first class appeals, and the careful and hard work, the police had insufficient evidence to bring charges against any of their suspects and they could not even be sure, with any degree of confidence, whether any of the three men was the individual responsible for the horrific crime.

The police identified a prime suspect. The man, who lived locally, was arrested and stood on an identity parade where he was picked out as a man who police believed may have been the killer, although it was not definite that he was involved in the crime. The suspect provided an alibi, however, and was released. Of course, people are often able to provide false alibis; Peter Sutcliffe did on a number of occasions during the hunt

for the Yorkshire Ripper. The police were satisfied that the man was not involved in the murder of Annie Walker and they were happy to let him go. He later committed suicide.

Locals still believe the man was responsible for the murder but police do not believe so. It is likely the killer was from Coalville rather than a resident of the close-knit village of Heather. Anyone living locally, who had come into such a substantial sum of money, would not have escaped the attention of the frightened and suspicious community, let alone the police. Equally, anybody who had such financial difficulties that would have spurred them into stealing the fortune in order to pay off debts, would have been quickly recognised, it is believed, had they lived in Heather. The small village community was one where people knew almost everyone's business and secrets were hard to keep.

Nine days after the murder, Detective Chief Superintendent Saunders praised the local community for their cooperation and for the information they had so far provided but he believed there was still potentially more information that could

Heather village school, temporarily used as a police station following Annie Walker's murder. The author

be brought to the attention of detectives who were still using the village school as their headquarters.

Reverend Clifford Berdinner spoke twelve days after the murder, of the crime being like a cloud over his parishioners and the fear that existed in the community. People did not venture outdoors at night as much as previously, he said, they locked up their doors earlier at night time and despite huge numbers of police officers continuously present in the village, a culture of fear prevailed.

The case went cold, with no further leads having been discovered, but with the advent of sophisticated forensic science techniques detectives gave hope to the people of Heather who still hope that the killer will be identified. In 2003, Leicestershire Police announced they had reopened the investigation and believed that DNA could provide a breakthrough.

An unidentified bloodstain was found on an item of clothing found at the scene of the crime and during the police review begun in 2003, nearly one hundred exhibits and pieces of evidence were analysed. These included an iron bar, clothing and fingerprints.

Forensic scientist Hazel Johnson said: 'Today, if we can go back to that bloodstain we should be able to get a DNA profile and come up with a profile of statistics of one in a billion.'

A DNA profile was obtained but even with this new significant evidence the police investigation has gone cold again. A check of the national DNA database failed to identify any match.

So who did kill Annie Walker? Was it the man who committed suicide, taking his secret to the grave, or was it some other, unidentified individual? More than forty years on the police believe they can still bring the killer to justice. Detective Inspector Jim Donaghty, an expert in unsolved serious crimes said: 'We will never give up trying to solve this murder.'

Detective Chief Inspector Mick Mills, the head of Leicestershire Police's cold case section, said: 'Despite the passage of time, Annie still requires justice and she still needs to be put to rest properly. 'Whether it's five years or fifty-five years ago, if it's unsolved then we'll keep revisiting and reviewing it to see of there's any further evidence.'

CHAPTER 9

Victim Unknown: Burton-on-Trent

c.1970

When David Nathan joined the Special Constabulary he hoped to be able to reduce crime and serve the local community. Few Specials are involved in investigating suspicious deaths, but a shooting expedition whilst not on service, led Nathan to almost literally stumble into one of the most intriguing mysteries that has perplexed police in Burton-on- Trent for decades.

It was the evening of Friday 26 March 1971 that the discovery was made on a small island covered with trees that divides the Newton Road Weir from the main stretch of the

The Spinney where the grisly discovery was made. The author

River Trent, approximately one mile from Burton on Trent town centre. Walking with his sporting gun and accompanied by his dog, Nathan left Newton Road and crossed a wooden footbridge approximately 150 yards away from the Newton Road recreation ground, and in close proximity to the old Mill, on to the Spinney, when something in the ground caught his attention. Looking closely at it he must have questioned what he thought he could see but the reality dawned upon him as he realised he had found a partially buried skull.

Naturally, Nathan alerted the police upon believing that it was human and the area was sealed off overnight. A careful and methodical excavation commenced at dawn of the following day, involving officers from across Staffordshire, under the direction of Assistant Chief Constable Harry Bailey. The painstaking excavation would eventually reveal the presence of the decomposed, skeletal remains of an adult, in a shallow grave beside a derelict kiln, covered in ashes.

As in all such cases rumours circulated the town, with the belief that the skeleton of a woman in her twenties had been discovered and police did nothing to dismiss such rumours, with Detective Chief Superintendent Harold Wright, who was originally in charge of the case, only informing the press that: 'We have located a skull and the top part of a torso, but we do not know yet if there is a complete body or whether it is in a standing, sitting or lying position. We are unable to say how long it has been here. It may be thirty years or much more recently.'

Many of the initial uncertainties would soon become clear, however, as the excavation was completed and medical examination of the remains commenced.

The remains were not of a historic nature; examination showed that they had been buried only up to approximately fifteen months earlier. A cause of death could not be determined, despite detailed medical examinations at Burton District Hospital centre, by local pathologists and Dr Keith Mant of Guy's Hospital, London, because the remains were so decomposed. There did not appear to be trauma to the skull, suggesting he had not been battered or shot. Due to the passage of time and the absence of flesh it could not be determined if

the man had been raped or subjected to a sexual assault or if he had been strangled.

The police quickly ruled that there were suspicious circumstances involved, not only because the man had been buried in a shallow grave in woodland but also because he was in a sitting position with his hands tied behind his back and his feet were also bound together. The man was naked except for a pair of mustard coloured socks. He was also wearing a gold wedding ring. It could never be determined if he had been killed where he was found, or if his dead body had been brought to that spot at a later time.

Murders, contrary to a popular belief generated by a sensationalist media, are relatively uncommon. Murders where the victim's identity is unknown are extremely rare in this country but this is the dilemma that Staffordshire Police had, and still have, in relation to this case.

Whilst the state of the remains made it difficult at the time of the discovery to provide a specific description of some aspects of the man's appearance the police are now able to give a general description of the man being white, aged twenty-three to thirty-nine, approximately 5' 8" tall with short brown hair, a prominent lower jaw and relatively small hands. There were, however, plenty of clues that could have led someone to recognise him. The man had upper dentures and extensive dental work on the teeth of his lower jaw within the final six months of his life. Further, he suffered from a rare medical condition known as torticollis which is a disorder affecting the neck, causing in this case the man's head to constantly lean to the right in a very noticeable manner.

Torticollis is caused by muscle spasms which cause the neck to twist. It is often called 'wry neck' and can be temporary or permanent, lasting only a few days before the sufferer returns to normal or gradually getting worse. It is normally confined to the neck, though some sufferers complain of it affecting the eyelids and vocal chords, and evidence suggests that it can run in families. Those suffering from the condition tend to be middle aged, though it can affect people of all ages. It is an uncommon disorder, affecting only three in every 10,000 people and can occasionally be caused by anti-psychotic drugs,

cocaine or amphetamines. It can also be caused by sleeping awkwardly or, when babies and infants are found to suffer from it, it can be caused by damage to the neck muscles during birth. In some cases no known cause can be identified.

This uncommon condition was not mentioned in the original appeals for information, presumably because it was not known that the victim suffered from torticollis, which may have contributed to the fact no one identified the deceased. Similarly, the earliest post-mortems suggested the man was aged thirty to thirty-five, an opinion well publicised, which would have hindered the investigation if indeed somebody knew of a twenty-three-year-old who had disappeared in 1969 or 1970.

Despite three years of extensive enquiries and high profile appeals in the early seventies, no one was able to come forward to tell police that they knew the dead man. Despite the major dental work, no dentists could recall having treated him as one of their patients. No one came forward to say their husband had gone missing and no one came forward to report a friend or loved one, with such a neck condition as the unidentified man, missing. Clearly, therefore, there is a strong probability that the man did not come from Burton-on-Trent, Staffordshire and quite possibly not even from the Midlands. Even if he had been killed by someone who wanted the man's identity to remain a mystery, medical staff in the area would have been aware of him had he been from the region.

At the time of the discovery the police did, as already stated, carry out an extensive investigation with numerous appeals for information about who the man was. However, they did so on a relatively local scale. Without the mass media that we have today it would have been virtually impossible to publicise the mysterious case across the nation; we still only had two television channels as opposed to the huge ongoing news presence available on our television screens. Without the Internet and without as high readership of newspapers as there is today news did not travel in the way we have become accustomed to. It is true to say that police across the country carried out checks of dental records and missing persons reports in their localities, the media outside of Staffordshire was largely uninterested, or unaware of this enigmatic case.

Times change though. In 2006, Staffordshire Police's Major Investigation Department in Lichfield began a cold case review in the hope of resolving the long-standing mystery surrounding the man's identity and, of equal importance, the identity of person or persons responsible for the unexplained death. It was hoped that fresh eyes and more modern policing techniques could lead to the breakthrough that had eluded them for decades. Recognising that they had been limited in 1971 in terms of publicising the enigma, detectives sought larger exposure and they turned to a resource that was years away from existence in 1971: *Crimewatch UK.*

By the time of the *Crimewatch* appeal an expert from the University of Dundee had created a digital reconstruction of the man's face, which was broadcast to millions of viewers across the country as well as being printed in local and national newspapers. It was also screened on television news in the Midlands and the national news programmes.

Detective Chief Inspector Dave Garrett, of the Staffordshire Police Major Investigation Department told the public: 'There could be someone, in Burton or anywhere in the UK, who had a husband, son or brother go missing in 1969 or 1970 who they've never traced. It is very rare for an unexplained death to remain unsolved in Staffordshire. We hope these new images may jog people's memory.'

Unfortunately the reconstruction did not jog any memories, or at least no one came forward with an identity for the man. Undeterred, in March 2008, the National Missing Persons Helpline renewed appeals for information, but to no avail.

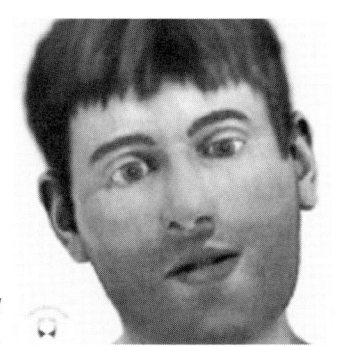

The facial reconstruction of the unidentified victim. Staffordshire Police/University of Aberdeen

There is, at least, one development in police work which may eventually help determine who the man is. A DNA sample has been taken from the remains and will be used if any possible relatives are traced.

If the man was married, as seemed to be the case with him wearing a wedding ring, why did his wife not report him missing, or his parents or neighbours, doctors or dentists? He had extensive dental care and his rare condition would have been known to his doctor, and there can be little doubt that he would have had some medical treatment for his torticollis.

Perhaps the man was not even British explaining why seemingly no one in this country knows his identity and explaining why no medical records matching this man's medical history are known to exist in this country. It could be that he was a migrant worker or illegal immigrant and there is something about his appearance from the reconstruction of the skull which hints at an East European origin, though like E-fits and police sketches, there is often an element of artistic license especially in skin tones and hair colour. If this is the case, the police have made a long standing error in concentrating their efforts in Britain.

Forty years or more after this man's death there are many questions and few answers. Who was this man, who killed him, how did he die and why was he killed? Why has no one come forward to identify the man and is there a family out there, somewhere in the world, desperately trying to locate a son, father or husband whose life was tragically ended in that small wooded area in Burton on Trent?

CHAPTER 10

Barbara Mayo: Ault Hucknall

1970

I t was on 18 October 1970 that a miner, by the name of Walter Krzyzanowski, and members of his family were walking through woodland at Ault Hucknall, near Chesterfield, approximately a mile off Junction 29 of the M1 and near the Derbyshire/Nottinghamshire border. Krzyzanowski walked ahead of his relatives, along a lover's lane, looking for chestnuts, and as he did so his attention was drawn to a pile of leaves. There was nothing particularly unusual about a large number of leaves on the ground, it being October. However, something was seen protruding from the leaves and, upon closer inspection, the decomposing body of a young female was revealed to the horrified miner who was sickened by what he saw.

The dead woman was fully clothed but her clothing had been disturbed. A post-mortem examination would later confirm that she had been viciously raped, battered around the head and strangled; strangulation having been the cause of death. The family, who were understandably shaken by the experience, marked the location with stones and two of them drove to the nearby Ault Hucknall Farm to contact the police. The body was, according to one of the family members, in an isolated location and, because of the falling of leaves from the trees, it could easily have been the case that her body would not have been found for many months. As it happened she had only been there a matter of days.

The victim was identified as Barbara Janet Mayo. Barbara was an attractive twenty-four-year-old schoolteacher from Hammersmith, south-west London. It had only been by chance that she found herself leaving London, on foot, to travel to Catterick. On Monday 12 October, six days before her body

was found, she had spoken to her boyfriend, David Pollard, whose car was being repaired in a garage in the North Yorkshire town. Barbara decided to hitchhike so that she could collect it and travel back to London. Barbara could drive, and she owned a car, but her own vehicle had been experiencing problems and she felt that relying on the goodwill of passing motorists would be a safer and more trouble-free means of travelling the approximately 250 mile journey.

Hitching a lift from one or more passing drivers was a far more frequently exercised method of travelling from A to B in 1970 than it is at present. In the twenty-first century the media's role in making people aware of murders and sexual assaults that have been taking place has resulted in a greater fear of crime and the belief that serious offences are more prevalent now than during the 1960s and 1970s. Barbara Mayo was an intelligent woman but one would imagine she would not have been too concerned by the thought of getting into a stranger's car and being driven across the country. With only two television channels and therefore a smaller number of news programmes than in modern times where channels are devoted to coverage of news stories, and fewer people reading the newspapers than at present, a crime such as that which happened to Barbara was something that many members of the public would never think would happen.

After leaving her home Barbara caught the tube from Hammersmith to Hendon and began thumbing a lift from there. David Pollard was never to hear from his girlfriend again and, concerned when Barbara failed to arrive back into London with the car, he reported her missing on 14 October. At this point in time, however, there was little concern for her safety among those outside of her family and friends.

However, the missing persons case had now become very serious and was a high priority. In the early hours of Monday 19 October more than thirty officers began to comb the scene of the crime and the surrounding woodland in the hope of finding some clue, no matter how seemingly insignificant on the face of it that the clue might seem. A white tarpaulin covered the area in which Barbara's body was found, and the search continued late into the night, aided by tall floodlights

attached to the roofs of police vans and a caravan. Despite the detailed search a bag belonging to Barbara, containing her purse and other small artefacts, which it is believed she would have certainly had with her, was never recovered. Did her killer take this because of the money within the bag or did he keep his victim's belongings as a trophy or memento of his crime?

The large scale of the manhunt was far greater than Derbyshire Constabulary, and the neighbouring Nottingham-shire Constabulary, were capable of dealing with. A far more experienced, larger police force was required to take control of the investigation. Detective Chief Superintendent Bradshaw, head of Derbyshire CID told journalists, so that a *speedy conclusion* could be reached. And so Detective Chief Superintendent Charles Palmer from Scotland Yard was given the unenviable task of leading the nationwide search for the man the tabloids were already dubbing *The Monster of the Motorway*. Even with his impressive track record of never having failed to solve a murder at that point in his career, and with the methods and manpower that the Metropolitan Police could afford to deploy, Palmer was under no illusion as to the nature of the challenge he faced.

The sheer number of motorists who travelled along Britain's roads, even in 1970, when a relatively tiny proportion of people were capable of driving when compared to today, meant that there were unmanageable numbers of suspects who each needed to be traced, interviewed and eliminated. Indeed it was estimated that more than 250,000 motorists were using the northbound carriageway of the M1 between the time Barbara left London, on Monday 12 October and Wednesday 14 October. Tracing each of these drivers, who were potential witnesses, was a mammoth task. During the course of the investigation 125,000 people were questioned, by 1,500 officers who took almost 50,000 statements, and the police still failed to find their killer. The national scale of the search, coupled with the finite resources available to the police force, and the lack of information known about the murderer, meant that the criminal had a greater chance of evading capture than the average predatory killer. What the police were expected to do was almost as difficult as attempting to capture a specific

Kimberley, where Barbara Mayo was arguably last seen alive. The author

fish by casting a small net in a vast ocean, when they were not even sure what the fish they were hunting for looked like.

There were, however, two witnesses whose evidence possibly placed Barbara less than twenty miles from Ault Hucknall. Both noted seeing a woman, who appeared to look very much like Barbara, in Kimberley, Nottinghamshire, which is located just off Junction 26 of the M1. The first witness, a butcher, seemed certain that on 12 October Barbara had walked into his shop on her own and had bought two freshly cooked faggots. Nothing struck him as unusual about the young woman's manner and, after purchasing the faggots, she walked out, crossed the road and walked down a hill towards a main road. The butcher did not believe there was anyone outside waiting for her.

The second witness reported seeing a woman matching Barbara's description seated in a Morris Minor 1000 Traveller car at Kimberley at around 4pm, also on 12 October. As Barbara had only left her flat in Hammersmith at 11.30am that day, travelled along the Underground before reaching the M1, could she have managed to hitch a lift and reach the Nottinghamshire town by 4pm? The police believed she could have done and they were fortunate in knowing that if the woman seen was indeed the murder victim then they had a fairly good description of the man driving the vehicle who, even if he was not the killer himself, he was one of the last people to see Barbara alive and therefore a very important witness. The man was described as being aged between twenty-five and thirty years, of medium build, with mousy hair brushed forward. The vehicle was seen travelling northbound towards the M1, which strengthened the police's belief that Barbara was the passenger and most probably her killer was the driver.

As part of their investigation police officers spoke to the drivers of each and every Morris Minor 1000 Traveller in the country, without the murderer's identity being determined. It is quite possible that the witness who made the sighting was incorrect in the belief that Barbara had been sighted and so the police had spent too many resources on a red herring. Barbara Mayo was a slim woman, five foot nine inches in height, with dark brown hair that went below her shoulders. The number of women who would have matched such a description would be huge and the height of the woman concerned would not have been able to be determined because she was seated in a car. Furthermore the witness was fully aware that someone else had believed they had seen Barbara in Kimberley and so this knowledge might have influenced the witness into believing that they too had seen the deceased when in reality they might have seen someone entirely different.

If the murdered schoolteacher was in Kimberley, however, and she was in the butcher's shop, then it would appear Barbara either felt at ease with her killer, for she was able to go into the butcher's on her own and did not make any effort to escape whilst presenting an ordinary demeanour rather than that of someone who had been held against her will, or it means that

whilst she was in Kimberley she had not yet met her murderer and instead was seeking another driver to take her the final distance to Catterick. The fact the woman crossed the road and walked towards a main road could suggest she needed to hitch another lift and so if indeed it was Barbara Mayo then it is possible the killer picked her up in Kimberley. Of course, the murderer could have parked out of sight, at some location on or near the main road, so that there were potentially fewer witnesses and Barbara could have been buying a faggot for herself and her killer, unaware of what was to happen. However, it is strange that he did not park closer to the shop when there were plenty of areas where he could have done so. It would appear, therefore, most likely that by the time she got to Kimberley Barbara had not yet met the man who was to end her life if it was she who was seen by the two witnesses.

The information provided by these witnesses, interesting though it was, did not lead to the breakthrough that was so desperately needed and despite the largest manhunt to have taken place in Britain at that time the killer's identity was as much of a mystery in the winter of 1971 when Palmer was reluctantly removed from the investigation, which gradually grinded to a halt, than it was in October of the previous year.

If the nationwide search for the Morris Minor was a waste of time it was not the only false lead that the police had to investigate. A man who took a bloodstained suit to a dry cleaners in the days following Barbara's murder was questioned. The suit belonged to the man's son and it had become bloodstained when the son had been involved in a car accident. Detectives were happy to eliminate both men from their enquiries. After all, Barbara was not cut or injured in any way that would have resulted in her blood having been transferred onto her killer's clothing. Even when the Yorkshire Ripper began his murderous acts Derbyshire Constabulary investigated the possibility that there could have been some connection between the mutilations of the prostitutes and the sexually motivated murder of Barbara Mayo. Upon being convicted of the Ripper murders in 1981, Peter Sutcliffe was formally questioned in connection with Barbara Mayo's death. It was known Sutcliffe owned a Morris Minor 1000 Traveller

and he had been in London around October 1970. In December 1997, however, Sutcliffe was finally eliminated from the investigation.

It has been frequently said over the years that motorists travelling in the region were stopped by the police and questioned over whether they could provide information. Whilst this it true the questioning of motorists did not begin until two weeks after Barbara had set out for Catterick. It is always important to speak to potential witnesses at the earliest possible stage but drivers who passed along the road, curious as to what the police were doing in the woods, were not questioned at all. A police reconstruction did not even take place until a further week later, by which time the memories of anyone who might have seen Barbara will have been affected. The police did put posters up in shops and businesses around Derbyshire but enquiries were not so strong in neighbouring Nottinghamshire even though it was almost certainly the case Barbara had been in that particular county with her killer having only driven slightly into Derbyshire to commit the murder and dump Barbara's body.

Despite a flood of telephone calls, with so many calls having been made that Chesterfield police had to obtain more telephone lines, no motorists ever came forward to say that Barbara had been their passenger and this is unusual because someone surely drove her out of London. Could this have been her killer, a man who drove her all the way from London to Derbyshire, or could it be that one or more innocent drivers, who had given her a relatively short lift, were too afraid of approaching the police in case they were incorrectly implicated in the crime? Indeed, the occupants of several cars, believed to contain 'courting couples', seen in a 'lovers lane' in the woods near where Barbara's body was found, made no efforts to contact the police.

The police assumed that Barbara had indeed been on her way to Catterick, and that she had set off on foot in the hope of being picked up by a passing driver, but Barbara's own mother had a different theory which could account for the lack of witnesses who had seen her in and around London. Marjorie Mayo believed the reason no motorists came forward was that

her daughter had been killed in London, probably by someone she knew, with her body having been dumped in Derbyshire in order to throw detectives off the killer's track. The reason for this belief was that on the day before she left for Catterick Barbara allegedly visited her mother and announced that she was very frightened about something. The cause of her concern will never be known because some visitors arrived which meant Marjorie could not address her daughter's concerns. However, surely if she had seemed very frightened indeed then the arrival of the visitors would not have discouraged Marjorie from talking to her daughter and she would have spoken to Barbara about the worries after the visitors had left. Perhaps the passage of time, and the knowledge of what happened to Barbara Mayo has meant that her mother's recollection of Barbara's manner was affected.

If Barbara was killed in Hammersmith, or elsewhere in London, then she could not possibly have been seen alive in Kimberley, could she? Was the butcher right to believe he had seen the dead woman or could he have been mistaken? Mistakes of identification are all too easy to make, as exemplified by the hundreds and thousands of people who in recent years have wrongly believed they have seen Lord Lucan and even Elvis Presley. However, there was never any evidential reason to doubt that Barbara had begun to hitchhike to North Yorkshire and on consideration of all the facts it would seem that she unsuspectingly got into her killer's car enroute.

The passing of the years has certainly allowed the killer to continue to evade justice and possibly live a normal life despite his wicked crime. However, the search for Barbara's killer has by no means ended. In 1997 Derbyshire Police obtained a sample of DNA from the dead woman's clothing and it is assumed that this genetic sample originated from the man who raped and killed her. Using the profile, which is undoubtedly the single significant clue the police have in their hunt to identify the killer, attempts have been made to trace each of the 250 original suspects and carry out DNA tests upon them.

At present all but a handful have been located and eliminated on the grounds that their DNA did not match. Officers have had to travel to as far away locations as Australia, New Zealand,

USA and Canada. It was as a consequence of comparing his DNA with the killer's DNA that enabled detectives to eliminate Peter Sutcliffe at the end of 1997. However, a difficulty has arisen in that police have been unable to take a sample from one man who currently lives in Canada because he has severe mental health problems and cannot consent to the tests. A legal challenge in the Canadian courts was undertaken in a bid to ensure that Derbyshire police were provided with some of the DNA belonging to the suspect.

It is all very well to eliminate the original suspects on the basis of DNA. However, if Barbara Mayo's killer was never considered to be one of the 250 suspects then other means of detection will have to be used if the police are ever to get close to solving this case.

In August 2001 detectives from Derbyshire Police made a televised appeal for information in the hope that one or more viewers would be able to offer a vital clue that would finally lay this case to rest. Sadly no significant pieces of information, or at least pieces of information that the police currently consider to be significant, were acquired through this means.

Those who campaigned for the release of Stephen Downing, the man jailed for murdering Wendy Sewell in 1973 in Bakewell but whose conviction was quashed in 2002, believe that Wendy Sewell and Barbara Mayo could very well have been killed by the same man. The evidence for this is not at all compelling, for Barbara was raped and strangled to death whilst Sewell was battered over the head and it would appear, despite Downing's confession when arrested in 1973, that no form of sexual assault took place. The bodies of both women were found to be in a star like position and their personal belongings had been stolen but it is here that the similarities end. Nonetheless it is true that suspects from the Sewell murder were questioned in relation to Barbara's death, because of the geographic and temporal proximity of the two attacks. Derbyshire Police have refused to accept there could be a link, however, and, partly as a result of Downing's taped confession following his release from prison, which he made before once again protesting his innocence, they believe Downing certainly did kill Wendy Sewell in the Bakewell cemetery. Nonetheless Downing did not

drive and it is known he did not play any role in the murder of schoolteacher Barbara Mayo.

Barbara was not the only victim of the *Monster of the Motorway*, however. A similar unsolved murder, this time in the nearby county of Cheshire, can be linked to the killing of Barbara Mayo. The partially clothed body of Jacqui Ansell-Lamb was found by a ten-year-old boy and his father as they walked through Square Wood, Mere, near Knutsford, just of the M6, on Sunday 8 March 1970. Jacqui, an eighteen-year-old secretary, had been hitchhiking from London to Manchester when she was sexually assaulted and strangled. Recent DNA examination of the clothing worn by Jacqui at the time of her death prove that both she and Barbara Mayo were killed by the same man. This had been suspected at the time but there was no evidence proving a link between the two crimes. Cheshire Police, like their Derbyshire colleagues, launched a massive police hunt involving 120 officers, but to no avail. They had received a 'good response', according to Chief Superintendent Arthur Benfield who headed the investigation but the killer remained free to strike again. On the weekend Jacqui was murdered, Manchester City were playing West Bromwich Albion in the League Cup Final at Wembley and 40,000 fans travelled to London to watch. Many of these fans will have been returning to Manchester, along the M6 on the day of the murder. Could Barbara Mayo and Jacqui Ansell-Lamb's killer have been one of them? The day before Barbara Mayo was murdered, Manchester City were playing away at Chelsea. Could the killer again have been returning from London, up the M1, when he came across Barbara? It is a possibility the police have not considered and which I uncovered during my research of this case.

Jacqui's killer may have driven a saloon car. A woman matching her description (Jacqui was wearing a blonde wig, false eye lashes, a dark blue maxi coat and maroon patent shoes) was seen getting into a saloon car at Keele services at between 4 and 5pm on the Sunday.

One has to wonder whether if Barbara was aware of Jacqui's death, and several other murders of hitchhikers that had taken place in the years preceding her own death, would she still have decided to hitch a lift to Catterick?

Peter Sutcliffe is not the only high profile killer whose name was briefly linked to the unsolved murder. Barbara Mayo and Jacqui Ansell-Lamb hit the headlines in November 2007 when Peter Tobin was arrested and charged in connection with the murder of Vicki Hamilton and has since been convicted. Tobin's house in Margate, Kent was used as a burial ground for two of his victims; Vicki Hamilton and Dinah McNicol, both of whom he killed in 1991.

Police briefly considered that Tobin might have been responsible for the murders of Barbara Mayo and Jacqui Ansell-Lamb, along with a list of other names of other murder victims and women who had gone missing. They do not believe, however, that he was responsible for the murder of the two hitchhikers in 1970.

There are huge differences, however, between the 1970 murders and those committed in 1991, not least that Barbara and Jacqui were both left near motorways and not buried in a garden or indeed buried at all. Dinah McNicol had been picked up on the A3 but money was withdrawn from her bank account in the weeks following her disappearance. Vicki Hamilton was last seen alive in Reading town centre where she was intending to catch a bus home.

In March 2008, another cold case seemingly became solved. Harvey Richardson died of cancer earlier that year, aged seventy-seven. Whilst decorating the Wigan property after his death decorators found a battered leather bag containing a nine page letter, which was handwritten on A5 paper that was yellowing with age, suggesting it had been written at least five or six years earlier (and probably decades earlier), and cuttings from a newspaper. The letter was a detailed confession to the murder of Lorraine Jacob who was murdered in Liverpool in September 1970, aged nineteen. The newspaper cuttings related to that murder but amongst them was a cutting relating to another case: the murder of Jacqui Ansell-Lamb.

Of course, there is no concrete proof that Richardson murdered Lorraine Jacob. It is a curious aspect of some human minds that they feel the need to confess to crimes they have had no involvement in. This has plagued my work in the field of miscarriages of justice and unsolved crimes for as long as I

have researched these cases, with me frequently receiving 'confessions' to the murder of Jill Dando from people who have come across my website and my writing. However, the level of detail contained within the letter has led to detectives in Liverpool believing strongly that Richardson may well have killed Lorraine and forensic evidence found at Richardson's home adds significant weight to the confession. An item of clothing was found with the confession and it has been speculated that this was either Lorraine's underwear or her tights, which were missing from her body. Lorraine's killer had taken the clothing as a 'trophy' just as Barbara's Mayo's killer had taken her handbag. The police have refused to confirm that the clothing in Richardson's bungalow had belonged to his alleged murder victim, but they concluded that forensic tests of items recovered from Richardson's home did point to him being the killer. Detective Superintendent Ian Kemble said the note, which was not signed or dated, 'quite accurately described as a confession to the murder of Lorraine in 1970'. Did the writer of the note also kill Jacqui and Barbara?

Like Barbara and Jacqui, Lorraine had been strangled to death. There was also evidence to suggest she had been sexually assaulted. She had been left in an alleyway rather than near the side of a motorway but Richardson had been living in Liverpool at the time, before moving back to Manchester where he was born, and so would have been able to dispose of Lorraine's body far more easily. He also lived in London and Bolton before moving to Wigan where he spent his final few years.

Interestingly Manchester City were playing in Liverpool, against Everton on the day before Lorraine Jacob was murdered. Is this an interesting coincidence or may it prove to be a sinister link connecting Richardson with three murders? Cheshire and Derbyshire Police do not believe that Richardson was involved in Jacqui or Barbara's murder, although they refuse to rule out the possibility. They refuse to confirm to me whether they have compared Richardson's DNA with the DNA found on Barbara and Jacqui. Detectives point to the fact that Richardson, who lived in Liverpool in 1970, never had a driving license when the murders were committed, and no one was aware that he had ever been able to drive, and therefore it is

highly unlikely he was responsible unless he had an accomplice, like so many sex killers often do. Personally I think the killer did have an accomplice; like Lorraine, Barbara and Jacqui did not have any other marks on them apart from the classic signs of strangulation and sexual assault.

A photograph issued by Merseyside Police, showing a bespectacled Harvey Richardson from 1966, bears an uncanny resemblance to the picture drawn of the man with whom Barbara was seen before her death. The Barbara Mayo murder suspect was not described as wearing glasses but from a distance these might not necessarily have been noticed. Having said that, police sketches of suspects are notoriously often inaccurate.

If Richardson had killed the two hitchhikers, would he not have mentioned the fact in his letter? After all, why confess to only one crime if you committed at least three? Why then did he have the newspaper cutting? Perhaps it was that reading about other similar crimes heightened his sexual gratification. Chillingly it may also be that the murder of Jacqui Ansell-Lamb inspired him to commit murder himself. Unless of course, he wrote the confession of only one murder because he had an attack of conscience about that one crime, perhaps when he heard that Lorraine had two children, but that he remained coldly nonchalant about the other two murders. The confession could have been written shortly after Lorraine's murder, before Barbara Mayo was killed and that might be the reason why Barbara's death was not confessed to. The fact is we can only speculate and Richardson could have been totally unconnected with the murder of Barbara Mayo and Jacqui Ansell-Lamb, even if he did take an unusual interest in the latter's death.

In January 2009, I was contacted by a man who claimed to have information about Barbara's murder. He informed me that he had been driving through Mansfield at some point in 1970, before the murder, when he saw a Morris 1000 Traveller with registration number TTV 454H. The reason he still remembers the number is because his own car of the time had a very similar number, he told me. Following the murder the man claims he saw a Vauxhall with the same registration number. When the man contacted the police regarding this he

A war memorial near to where Barbara is thought to have bought food. The memorial reads 'Their Name Liveth For Ever More.' The name of Barbara's killer is an ongoing mystery. The author

was dismissed because that registration number was recorded as being for an Austin Princess but to this day the man remains adamant that his recollection is accurate. Was the Morris 1000 Traveller with registration TTV 454H ever located and its

owner eliminated? Was this vehicle in anyway connected to the crime? Or could the man simply be mistaken?

Nearly four decades may have elapsed since Barbara Mayo's life was untimely ended and Derbyshire Constabulary have once again scaled down their search for the elusive killer. However, the file in this unsolved murder case remains wide open and now that DNA evidence is available there is new hope that the man who committed this evil act could, if he is still alive, one day stand in the dock, before a judge and jury, accused of one of the most heinous unsolved murders to have taken place in Derbyshire.

CHAPTER 11

Judith Roberts: Tamworth

1972

The case of Judith Roberts is unusual in that a man was arrested, tried and convicted for her murder. Indeed, Andrew James Evans confessed to committing the crime and served twenty-five years in prison, most of this time having accepted guilt, before being sensationally cleared at the Court of Appeal following protestations of innocence.

Judith Roberts was fourteen years old when she was killed in the early evening of 7 June 1972. She had decided to ride her bicycle around the country lanes near her home in Tamworth, Staffordshire, just a few miles from the Derbyshire border. When she failed to return home, her parents were besides themselves with worry and even their worst fears will not have compared with what was to be recognised as to the reality of what had happened to the teenager.

It was three days later before Judith's body was found, under a pile of hedge clippings and plastic fertiliser bags, close to a hedge in a field known as Robinson's field. The bicycle was found within the hedge, just a few feet away. The high profile murder hunt failed to achieve the response that detectives were looking for. This would change months later, however.

Although Judith, the daughter of a schoolmaster, was found laying face down with the bottom half of her clothing removed, there was no sign of rape or sexual assault. Death was, however, a violent one; a post-mortem examination revealed nineteen wounds on the schoolgirl's head, one of which was a heavy blow to the back of the head resulting in her skull being fractured so much so that the brain was damaged. It is believed that this injury was the cause of death and it was also the initial blow, inflicted whilst the girl was stood up rendering her unconscious

immediately upon being struck, with the killer then having struck needlessly eighteen more times.

There followed a large and widespread police investigation with coverage on a national scale, provoking fear and concern amongst the local population.

It was not until October that the police made what they believed to be a breakthrough in the case, when seventeen-year-old Andrew Evans approached officers to tell them that he believed he might have been responsible for the crime. In fact he presented entirely inaccurate information about the murder but would soon become the only suspect in the case.

Evans was, at the time of Judith's death, a soldier serving in Whittington Barracks near Lichfield, which is only four miles away from the scene of the crime. He had only been serving in the army since April 1972, having been somewhat of a failure in life. He wanted to prove to those who knew him that he had it in him to make something of himself and so he joined up to fight for Queen and country in pursuit of respect. Once again he failed, leaving the army on medical grounds after suffering quite a severe asthma attack during a training run. He was discharged from the army on 8 June 1972 and returned to his parents' home before moving in with his grandmother.

Due to the fact he had recently left the army he was asked to attend the local police station to fill in a form asking him where he had been between 6pm and 10.30pm on the day Judith Roberts was murdered. Evans recalled on his form that he had been: 'In barracks and never left on this date. Was discharged the next day on medical grounds suffering with asthma.' He supplied the names of three soldiers who, he said, could substantiate this alibi.

Evans' renewed feeling of failure resulted in the onset of depression and his GP prescribed him with valium on 29 September 1972. By this point in time Evans had not expressed any interest in the murder. This was, however, soon to change when he was visited out of the blue by the police.

On the evening of Sunday 8 October 1972, officers investigating the killing of Judith Roberts visited Evans at his grandmother's home to question him in relation to the murder. It had transpired that two of the three soldiers whom he had

believed could offer an alibi were no longer serving at the barracks by the time of the murder, and they had been unable to locate the third soldier.

Although Evans wrote a statement in which he reiterated his claim that he had been in the barracks at the time of the murder, he was highly disturbed by the questioning and began to question whether he had been involved in the crime. Although he did not suggest he had been the killer, whilst the police were present, he did ask the officers what would happen to the murderer if he was caught. The response given was that the killer would be in considerable trouble and would need his head examining. After the police left his grandmother spent much of the evening attempting to reassure the worried man, who was by this stage very worked up and agitated, that he had not killed the teenager. This did not, however, prevent him from visiting the police the following day after a sleepless night.

The following morning Evans told his grandmother that he needed to speak to the police and see a photograph of the victim in order to try and recall whether he was responsible for her death. When he arrived at Longton Police Station at around 3pm he told a police cadet that he kept dreaming about a girl. When taken to see a Detective Sergeant, Evans was inconsolable, sat with his head between his knees and his hands on his face.

When he had calmed down he told the detective he needed to see a photograph of the victim, adding: 'I was in the Army, I don't remember where I was.'

After being asked more questions, he was taken to see a Detective Inspector whom he told he was very upset because: 'It is this girl who was murdered at Tamworth. I keep seeing a face. I want to see a picture of her. I keep seeing her face. I wonder if I've done it.'

Evans was then asked details about the crime and the victim. He provided vague details of the girl's face but a very inaccurate description of her clothing. Upon being asked whether he believed he had 'done it', the new suspect announced, 'I don't know whether I've done it or not ...' Asked whether he had ever been to Tamworth, he replied, 'I don't know. I don't know. I

could have done. I forget where I've been. I can go down streets and in houses and later I wonder how I got there.'

He was then asked about his activities after leaving the army, to which he replied: 'You see, I can't remember. This is how I am. I could have got home the next day. I don't know where I've been. That is why I keep wondering if it's me that's done this murder. Can you show me a picture to see if I've ever met her?'

He was then asked again if he had killed Judith Roberts, responding: 'This is it. I don't know. Show me a picture and I'll tell you if I've ever seen her.'

At 3.30pm the interview ended, though he remained at the police station and was questioned at 4.15pm by a Detective Chief Inspector and a Detective Constable. He reiterated his demand to see a photograph of the girl but this time announced he believed he had killed the victim: 'I keep seeing her face all the time. I can't sleep. I've got to know if I did it because I think I must have done.'

'I must have killed her,' he later repeated in a hysterical state. Soon afterwards Evans was cautioned and taken to Tamworth Police Station. Whilst at Tamworth he was questioned by one of the detectives who had visited him at his grandmother's home. He was asked by the Detective Sergeant whether he was the killer. 'I think so. I must have done because I can see a picture of her. I can see her lying near to a hedge. I can see her brown hair and she has got a mark across her face,' he replied. The mark, he believed, was a wound with blood. Evans then, in a confused state, claimed he had not committed the crime but he may have witnessed the attack and he offered a description of a man he said was the killer, telling the detective it was a small youth around 5' 4" in height, with dark hair.

He was asked a series of questions, his responses being accurate in some cases but largely inaccurate. He drew a picture of the crime scene which bore no resemblance to the field and showed the victim laying on her back.

The following day he told officers, whilst not under caution, he had dragged the victim from her bicycle and that there had been a struggle, adding that he believed he may have put the bicycle in the hedge.

Shortly afterwards he told detectives 'I am sure I killed her,' before asking them in a confused state, 'Do you think I did it?'

Later in the afternoon he told an officer, 'I know I did it. I've put it down,' before giving the officer three sheets of paper with detailed descriptions and drawings of the crime. The account gave information about a struggle with the girl and reiterated his inaccurate belief that she had been laying on her back. Late that night he provided a further four sheets of paper containing details of his belief of his actions on the fateful day. He was transferred to Lichfield police station and questioned about the contents of the sheets of paper, providing a detailed description of the weapon he allegedly used in the attack.

The following day he provided two more sheets which included a picture of a girl with no face. He added that the girl had had no clothes on after the attack and that he had left the victim under the hedge, when in reality she was half-clothed and had been left near the hedge, under hedge clippings.

During later police questioning it is alleged he provided details of the girl's appearance which only the killer, or someone who had been given information, could know. This was, for the police, sufficient evidence of his guilt despite the largely inaccurate information he had provided and his general confusion about his involvement in the crime. He was taken on a reconstruction of the movements he believed he made on the day of the murder, by a Detective Sergeant from the Metropolitan Police, whom he told: 'I want all this cleared up. If I don't receive some treatment I may do it again. I don't want that to happen.' Evans appeared to know the area around Robinson's field reasonably well, though he later accounted for this by saying he had been running in the area during training with the army.

Later that day Evans told the police he had a clear recollection of the handlebars and seat of the bicycle sticking out of the hedge as he left the scene of the crime. In fact the handlebars and seat were not visible. He made a detailed statement, which he signed, giving a full account of his alleged actions. Many of the details of the account matched the facts as the police understood them. Other information provided by the suspect, however, had no foundation and differed greatly from the truth.

The inaccuracies, however, were insufficient to dissuade the officers from believing they had their man and so, the following day, 12 October 1972, Evans was formally arrested and charged with the murder. Earlier that day he had told detectives: 'I told you. I killed her. I don't want it to happen again. I'll help you all I can. You must believe me now. I've told you what I did.' Upon being charged he reaffirmed this claim, saying: 'Yes … I did it.'

At his appeal in 1997, Evans' legal team argued that if their client had had access to a solicitor and doctor it would have been clear that he was not fit for questioning and that anything he had said could not be viewed to be credible due to his severe state of confusion. They alleged that even his trial had been used by Evans as 'an exercise to see for himself whether he was guilty. He did not know if he was guilty.' Indeed, prior to his trial Evans told Dr Washbrook, the prison medical officer at Winson Green, that he would be very disappointed if he did not stand trial, because he wanted to know whether he had committed the murder. Washbrook discovered that Evans was suffering from amnesia probably resulting from trauma, which may have only been the questioning that had taken place by detectives at his grandmother's house, the consequences of which it is argued would, due to the nature of Evans' character, have been significantly distressing so as to create intense stress levels and even amnesia.

It was whilst on remand that evidence was uncovered suggesting Evans' confessions could not be deemed to be reliable. Dr JF Scott, a consultant psychiatrist found that the accused 'showed no evidence of quick temper and appeared anxious to volunteer as much information as he could remember'.

He decided that a truth drug be used to uncover information that Evans had appeared to have forgotten. Both the defence and prosecution teams agreed that this be an appropriate course of action. Barbiturate drugs were administered, followed by intense questioning, on Friday 30 March 1973. During the course of this action Evans said he had been at the barracks throughout the day of the murder. He did however say that he had witnessed a man standing over the body of

Judith Roberts. He described barbed wire and a sign and recalled the name 'Brookes'. When asked if he killed Judith Roberts he answered: 'I don't know' and 'I didn't do it,' before saying, 'I must find out' and asking 'Was it me?'

A few days later, on 2 April, he was injected with Brietal and given Methedrine, with the hope that it would generate thoughts and improve recollection. Yet again he told detectives he had not left the barracks all day but admitted he knew the area where the crime was committed, but only because police officers had taken him there and because he had been there during his military training. He said he had never seen the victim and had played no role in her death. Against the advice of Dr Washbrook, a third session was undertaken in which Evans gave a detailed description of a man whom he said was the killer.

At the trial in 1973, however, the jury were led to believe that the defendant was suffering from amnesia, which had been caused by Evans trying to blank from his mind either having personally killed Judith Roberts, or having witnessed the crime. Evans and his defence argued, however, that he had not been present at the crime scene and that he was in fact in the barracks all of the day and night on which Judith was killed, as per his original statements. The apparent strength of his many confessions, however, proved ample evidence for the jury to convict. This was in spite of there having been no eyewitnesses to the crime, no forensic evidence, and indeed the clothing that Evans would have worn had he been the killer was returned to the army and contained no bloodstains or damage consistent with him having battered a girl to death and indeed struggle with her.

Needless to say, the jury failed to see the significance of the lack of evidence and they understandably concentrated on the confession, duly reaching a guilty verdict. Evans made no attempt to launch an appeal and spent eighteen years in prison, progressing through the penal system to such a point that he eventually became eligible for home visits and was serving his sentence in an open prison. It was at this stage that he began to protest his innocence and was immediately returned to a closed prison. A campaign to clear his name was launched and

expert opinions were sought to question the reliability of his confession, the fact that he had not been cautioned during some of the periods of police questioning and that he had been denied access to a solicitor and doctor.

Those campaigning for Evans, however, were not the only ones to raise concern about the confession evidence. In October 1997, a report commissioned by the prosecution for the appeal hearing, written by Dr Joseph, stated: 'I believe that when the appellant [Evans] was in the police station on Monday 9th October 1972 onwards, he was in a highly abnormal mental state. When he described 'seeing' the face of the dead girl I believe he is describing what would be categorised as a pseudo-hallucination, namely an abnormal perceptual experience ... I believe that the appellant was in a markedly anxious and "hysterical" frame of mind and it is not uncommon in such a state for a sufferer to believe that they can see things ... Taking into account the appellant's abnormal mental state and the way he was presenting himself at the police station, if I had been the psychiatrist examining him at that time or soon afterwards, I would have started off from the basic premise that the "memory" and imagery that he was describing were false and not true. I believe however that the psychiatrists who saw him at that time started from the opposite premise, namely that the memory and imagery the appellant was describing were true but incomplete.'

Dr Joseph further reported that Evans 'has a tendency to confabulate to fill in gaps in his memory, and the effect of psychiatric intervention at that time was to reinforce the belief that he was suppressing a real memory rather than what I believe to have been the correct analysis, namely that he had been experiencing a pseudo-hallucination and false memory as part of his extreme anxiety and "hysterical" state, which he subsequently elaborated with police and psychiatric encouragement. I believe therefore that his confession is unreliable.'

Dr Joseph's view was shared by three other experts in the field and the appeal judges who, in their judgment, found that the confessions were 'entirely unreliable'.

The appeal raised many contradictions between Evans' account and what actually happened. Evans was wrong in his

description of the direction in which Judith was cycling. He was wrong in his claim that he had dragged Judith off her bicycle and across rough terrain, for the killer did not do this. He was wrong in saying that he struck a blow to her head and continued struggling with her, because the medical evidence proved that the first blow had killed her outright. He was wrong in his description of the murder weapon. He was wrong in saying that he inflicted all of the blows when Judith was on the ground, because the medical evidence showed she was stood up when the first blow was struck. He was wrong about where in the field the attack took place. He was wrong about undressing the victim and putting her shoes in her underclothes. He neglected to give any description of hiding the body under hedge clippings and plastic fertiliser bags, despite giving several detailed accounts of his alleged behaviour. And he gave inaccurate information about the appearance of his alleged victim and the clothes she was wearing. Whilst some of his information was accurate, it was not a difficult task undermining his confessions, and it has been suggested he obtained information from the police by the questions they asked him.

So, with Evans' confession out the window, and his conviction overturned, the police had to start their investigation once again, at a disadvantage of twenty-five years. What leads did they now have?

As has been stated, there were no known witnesses to the crime, unless Evans himself was a witness but his accounts are, it has been shown, entirely unreliable. Also, no one has been identified who had reason to kill Judith. It was, presumably, a stranger murder.

The examination of the victim's bicycle revealed an unidentified fingerprint. None of Evans' fingerprints were found on the bicycle. Did the print belong to Judith's killer? Checks of prints on record failed to identify who the print belonged to.

At appeal, the judges argued that the police investigation into Andrew Evans had been somewhat questionable: 'Judged by the rules and standards of today, the conduct of this investigation by the police left much to be desired: the appellant

was not cautioned as and when he should have been, as is accepted by the Crown; he was not seen by a doctor when he first appeared at the police station, although it is clear that by current standards medical attention was urgently required; he was not offered the assistance of a solicitor.' Of course, the flawed police investigation and the treatment of Evans, is not an indicator of his innocence.

Was Evans the killer of Judith Roberts, despite his confusion and unreliable confession? Did he witness the murder? Or was he a fantasist and confused individual who had no involvement whatsoever in the crime? Did Evans see a small youth or was it a figment of his imagination? Was Evans even in the barracks on the day of the crime? These are questions that continue to have no definite answers. Just because he provided an unreliable confession does not mean the confession was not based on some element of truth and fact. A quashed conviction is no more a testament to innocence as a 'not guilty' verdict at the end of a criminal trial; it is simply a sign that there is insufficient evidence pointing to guilt and suspicions that the accused might be innocent. However, without the confession there was no evidence against Evans and it is probable that he was in Whittington Barracks at the time of the crime.

'Today is the first step to a life beyond injustice,' Evans declared as he left the Court of Appeal. 'This verdict means that my long nightmare is finally over,' he said. The nightmare for Judith Roberts' family, however, continues with the knowledge that their sense of injustice remains unresolved with the culprit having not been held to account. In the years after his release, Evans was awarded a total of nearly £1 million in compensation for the twenty-five years he spent in prison but the family of the murdered schoolgirl once again live their lives with the pain of knowing their daughter's murder remains unsolved. One has to wonder whether, if Evans is as seems innocent, had he not confessed to the terrible crime, would Judith Roberts' killer have got away with murder for nearly forty years?

CHAPTER 12

Wendy Sewell: Bakewell

1973

N o book about unsolved murders in and around Derbyshire would be complete without the high profile case of Wendy Sewell. I do not wish to discuss the controversial conviction of Stephen Downing in great detail because to do so would be to only repeat what has already been written about countless times before, most notably by Don Hale. I will devote discussion to the crime itself. It will, of course, be necessary, however, to give an overview of the conviction and appeal of Downing and the reinvestigation (Operation Noble) conducted by the police after Downing's conviction was overturned in January 2002.

Whilst controversy surrounds this case, as it does with most of the convictions overturned by the Court of Appeal, there do remain two facts: first, that Wendy Sewell was murdered and second, that the identity of the killer remains a mystery and is

Shock and horror spread through the whole town of Bakewell following the murder and remains a topic of conversation. The author

open to debate. As far as the judicial system is concerned, Wendy Sewell's murder is unsolved and there is strong evidence pointing to some unknown individual having been responsible for tragically ending her life.

Wendy Sewell was a thirty-two-year-old typist, working for the Forestry Commission at Catcliffe House, King Street, in Bakewell. On the day she was attacked, Wendy had decided to use her lunch break to visit the local cemetery. The reasons for this have been the subject of the controversy, with the suggestion that she was intending to meet a secret lover at the location, but the view accepted by the police is that she was intending to study the gravestones, her father having been buried in an unmarked grave in Sheffield. According to Wendy's mother, the two had discussed buying a gravestone and Wendy had said she would have a look at designs.

Whatever the reason for her visit to the cemetery, it was at this location that her killer struck on 12 September 1973. Wendy was seen walking alone from her place of work, up Butts Road towards the cemetery. She began the walk at around 12:40pm and was seen entering the cemetery ten minutes later.

The main entrance to the cemetery. The author

The lower path, where Wendy Sewell was violently attacked. The author

At some point in the next half hour, Wendy was attacked in the grounds of the cemetery. During the broad daylight attack she was struck about the head with a blunt instrument at least seven times. This caused severe head injuries including fractures to the skull. Her face, hair, hands and lower stomach were covered in blood. Her trousers, pants, plimsolls and bra had been removed by her killer. A pickaxe handle, bloodstained and splintered, was found a short distance away along with the bloodstained garments.

It was Stephen Downing who found the semi-conscious victim as she lay bleeding to death. Downing worked for the local council, doing odd jobs at the cemetery. He calmly went to see the cemetery attendant, Wilfred Walker, to report what had happened and seek help. The police and other members of staff were soon at the lower path, where the crime had taken place.

Downing claims he was at home at the time of the fatal attack, on his lunch break. He claims that at 1pm he left the cemetery to return to his nearby home, with the intention of

feeding two hedgehogs he had found, and have some lunch with his mother, though upon his arrival he learnt the animals had already been fed. Whilst walking to his house he claims he saw Wendy Sewell near woodland adjacent to the cemetery. Five witnesses saw Downing leave the cemetery, walking in his normal manner. Others claim they saw Wendy Sewell alive after Downing had left, though the police have doubts regarding the statements provided by these witnesses. If Downing was guilty it was accepted that he must have killed Wendy before leaving the cemetery.

At around 1:20pm Downing claims he left home to return back to work and found Wendy dying approximately five minutes later, at which point he went for help. He went back with three workmen who saw Wendy struggling and trying to stand. At one point she managed to stand up before falling and banging her head on a gravestone. It is quite possible that it was the fall that eventually killed her.

Wendy Sewell managed to survive for two days after the horrific attack, dying at Chesterfield Royal Hospital as a result of the injuries she sustained. She was not, however, in a fit state to be able to offer any information relating to her killer or the crime, having slipped into a coma soon after her arrival at the hospital.

The police soon identified their suspect, however. Stephen Downing was arrested, questioned until 11.10pm on the day of the attack and charged with assault after signing a confession. Two days later, when Wendy died from her injuries, Downing's charge was elevated to one of murder. Whilst on remand he retracted his confession and stood trial at Nottingham Crown Court where a jury convicted him of murder on 15 February 1974, after considering their verdicts for only one hour. An attempt to appeal on the basis of a new witness who claimed she saw Wendy Sewell alive and well whilst Downing was at home, on his lunch break, was not seen as credible grounds to allow his release and Downing's case slipped into obscurity for much of the next twenty-seven years.

In February 2001, Stephen Downing was successful in a high profile campaign, led by the former *Matlock Mercury* editor Don Hale, to secure his release from prison. He was released

on bail pending an appeal which took place in January the following year. The appeal was uncontested and so ended one of the longest miscarriages of justice in British criminal history.

The claims that Downing did not kill Wendy Sewell were based on more than just a 'legal technicality' contrary to popular belief. Downing, who had the reading ability of an eleven-year-old and was a naïve and immature individual at the time of his arrest at the age of seventeen, claimed from an early stage, albeit a few weeks after being charged, that his confession was not genuine. Indeed, campaigners such as Don Hale have alleged that the vocabulary and phraseology used in the confession could not possibly have been used by the mentally retarded suspect. Further, the confession was highly inaccurate; Downing claimed to have struck Wendy twice but her killer had hit her at least seven times and, probably, many more times than that. Downing claimed to have sexually assaulted the victim but there was no evidence of sexual assault.

Downing alleges he was deprived of food and sleep, being questioned into the late hours of the night. He claims he was confused and it is indisputable that he was not offered the services of a doctor or solicitor. It is now law that a suspect who has a mental or psychological illness, or is suspected of having such, be provided with a doctor or social worker or some other appropriate adult. This was not the case in 1973, however. Nonetheless it was law that a suspect be informed that he or she was entitled to the presence and advice of a solicitor. Stephen Downing was not cautioned upon his arrest and received no such offer of legal representation. Downing also claims that he only confessed to assaulting Wendy because he felt that she had not been seriously injured. Indeed she was still alive when he was being questioned and he apparently did not realise that by confessing he was admitting to such a serious offence and he confessed to grievous bodily harm, naively believing the consequences of doing so would be more tolerable than enduring an ongoing interview in the expectation that Wendy would live to tell the police that Downing was not the man who attacked her.

Prior to his trial, Downing offered the following statement regarding his confession:

I was taken to the police station at 2.00pm. They started to question me and kept me until 11.00 pm. I kept denying that I had done it. Eventually I got very tired and I started dropping to sleep. They said they would carry on all night with questions. Eventually I admitted to the attack. I did this because I was tired and wanted to get some sleep. Later, during the time I was being questioned, the police never threatened me but they did get hold of me by my shoulders and shake me because I wouldn't admit it. I asked if I could see my parents. At first they said 'no', but eventually my parents came. I asked my dad if I needed a solicitor but one of the policemen said I didn't. I had blood on the knees of my jeans and possibly on the soles of my feet. That got there whilst I was kneeling on the floor at the side of Wendy Sewell.

Upon careful examination of the available evidence, the Court of Appeal decided that the confession evidence was inaccurate and entirely unreliable. It had, it was determined, been extracted using questionable police techniques and it should not have been used as evidence proving Downing's guilt. This is especially the case as he retracted it.

'The safety of this conviction depends on the reliability of confessions made to the police on 12th September 1973. The court cannot be sure that the confessions were reliable. It follows that the conviction is unsafe,' the appeal judges ruled in 2002 when quashing the conviction.

The other main evidence against Downing was the presence of heavy bloodstaining of his clothing. One might expect him to be heavily bloodstained if he had quite innocently found Wendy Sewell whilst she was bleeding profusely. Wendy was also seen shaking her head quite violently when Downing was nearby, in the presence of others who were trying to assist her. She tried standing up at one point and was moving almost constantly. Blood could, therefore, have been transferred during such movements.

At the trial, Mr Lee for the prosecution, told the court that the bloodstaining on Downing's trousers and boots: '... might well be described as a textbook example of the pattern of bloodstaining which might be expected on the clothing of the

assailant in a wounding such as that which Wendy Sewell suffered.'

A similar claim was made in the trial of Sion Jenkins two decades later. Jenkins was convicted of killing his foster daughter largely on the basis of bloodstaining on his clothing. Jenkins always maintained he had found Billie-Jo Jenkins as she laying bleeding to death but the presence of thousands of small and microscopic spots of blood allegedly proved his involvement in the crime itself. This claim was later shown to be incorrect with new evidence showing the blood could have been transferred whilst he tried to help his dying stepdaughter after she was attacked. Jenkins' conviction was overturned on the strength of this evidence.

Similarly, in the Wendy Sewell murder, the presence of bloodstaining on Downing's clothes was shown to be quite probably of an innocent nature. He had been immediately next to her, after all. Mr Stockdale, a forensic scientist commissioned for the successful appeal hearing produced a report to the effect that the presence of blood such as that on Downing's trousers and boots was as consistent with his claim of finding the body after the attack as it was consistent with the claim he had been responsible for the attack. The bloodstain evidence, therefore, was neutral and did not prove anything one way or the other. An independent witness also cast doubt on the prosecution's case at trial allowing the appeal judges to reach the conclusion that: 'It is clear that the evidence of bloodstaining cannot now be relied on in support of a submission that the conviction was safe.'

The experts were not unanimous in their opinions, however. Mr J Fraser, Head of Kent Police Forensic Investigation, also carried out an examination of Downing's clothing in preparation for the 2002 appeal. He concluded: 'The pattern of bloodstaining on Stephen Downing's clothing supports the assertion that Stephen Downing battered Mrs Sewell prior to handling and kneeling by her body.'

However, bloodstaining evidence is not an exact science. It often comes down to human interpretation and it is impossible to replicate scenarios in which the process of blood transfer took place. It is therefore not always accurate. The blood was

predominantly concentrated on the knee of Downing's clothing, with small amounts of blood on the rest of his clothing and on his hands, consistent with him having knelt in blood and having only briefly come into contact with the victim such as by turning her over as he claimed to have done, rather than having subjected her to a violent beating, stripping her and carrying out a sexual assault. This is in contrast to the ambulance staff who were heavily soaked in Wendy's blood, much in the same way that her killer must have been. The forensic evidence itself cast doubt on Downing's guilt and introduced the possibility of some unknown individual having been responsible for the brutal murder for which Downing had spent twenty-seven years in prison.

No DNA other than that from the victim's blood was found on the murder weapon. There was a partial handprint and partial fingerprint on the pick axe handle, neither of which belonged to Stephen Downing or any of the other suspects. However, these prints could have come to be on the handle from any point in time, with the handle having been contaminated over the years. It was not stored in good conditions and it has been handled by countless individuals. The prints could be entirely unrelated to the crime. Unfortunately the handle was not examined for fingerprints in 1973. Textile fibres which did not originate from Downing's clothing were also found on the murder weapon though again these could have come to be on the handle at any point in time.

Taking the unreliable confession out of the equation, the only evidence implicating Downing in the attack that cost Wendy her life consisted of blood on his clothing.

With no eyewitness evidence, no fingerprints or forensic evidence linking Downing to the crime, and the only suggested motive that he had to kill Wendy being that he had never had a girlfriend, the case against Downing is eroded to the point that the case against him is now incredibly tenuous. Downing was present at the scene of the crime, shortly after the crime, that much is fact. How long he had been there is open to debate. However, there is nothing directly linking him to the crime.

So if Downing did not kill Wendy Sewell, who did? Operation Noble, the police reinvestigation into the murder of Wendy

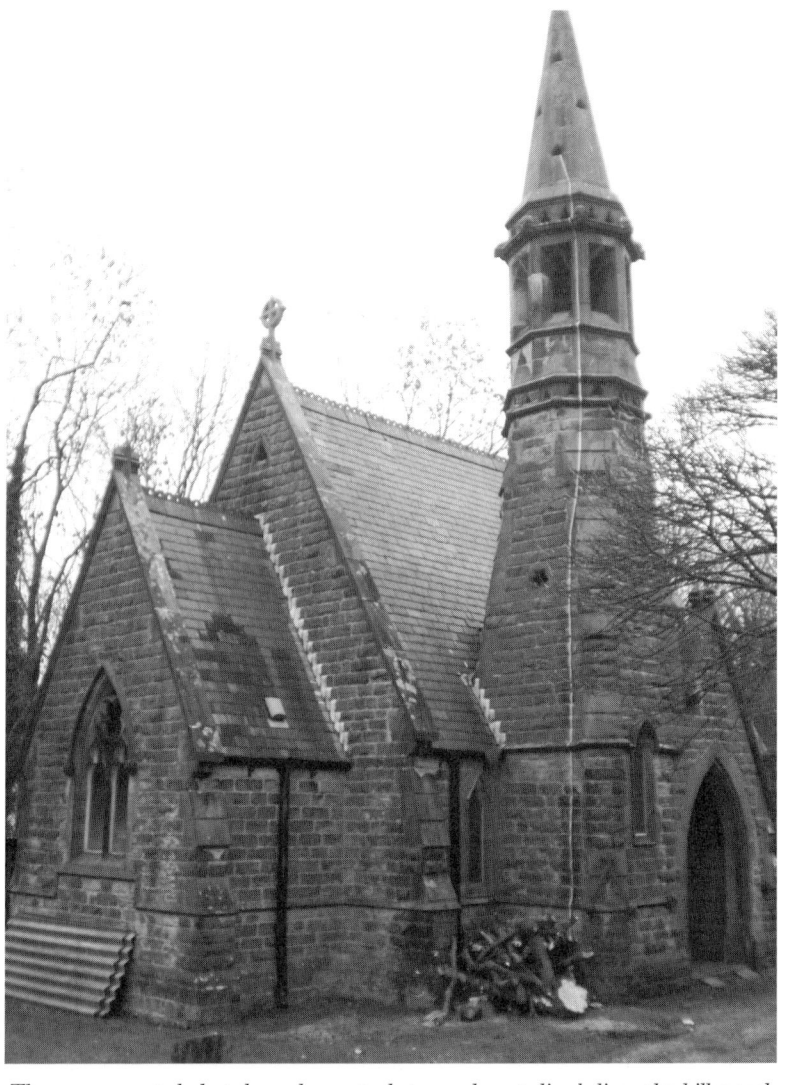

The unconsecrated chapel, used as a tool store, where police believe the killer took the murder weapon. The author

Sewell, followed 2,000 lines of enquiry, with 2,600 documents being examined, 360 new witnesses identified and 245 new witness statements obtained. In total twenty-three suspects were identified, which included Stephen Downing, Downing's father, Wendy's husband and a number of Wendy's alleged

lovers and former lovers. Essentially everyone known to have been around the cemetery at around the time of the murder was considered a suspect, including those who worked there. A man who sexually assaulted and killed a woman in Glossop, Derbyshire, in 1978 was also considered a suspect. Due to the rare nature of such crimes a potential link was investigated. The convict, however, was in hospital on the day Wendy Sewell was attacked. There was no evidence of him having ever had any connection to the victim or indeed Bakewell.

Another man, suspected of killing Barbara Mayo, found himself to become a suspect in the reinvestigation into the murder of Wendy Sewell. The man, however, was found to have been in prison at the time of Wendy's attack. It would appear he is also innocent of any involvement in the death of the hitchhiker killed in 1970.

The murder of Barbara Mayo was very different to that of Wendy Sewell although Don Hale believes there are similarities which should warrant great consideration of a possible link, especially if the killer's DNA can be obtained from Wendy's clothing. However, my research suggests another possible link worth considering; only one year earlier, of course, Judith Roberts was battered to death between thirty and thirty-five miles away. Both Wendy and Judith had their clothing disarranged and articles of clothing removed. Both may have possibly been sexually assaulted but there was certainly sexual motive behind the crimes. And both had been killed in an almost identical manner. The only differences were the ages of the victims and the fact Judith's killer had covered his victim whilst there had been no effort to hide Wendy's body, though realistically there would have been insufficient time to do so in a public place in broad daylight and there was nowhere to hide the body anyway. The police never considered a link, because Andrew Evans was already in prison by the time of the Bakewell murder. I believe there are grounds to consider the distinct possibility that Judith and Wendy may have been killed by the same man.

One unfortunate man was implicated in Wendy's murder by vindictive relatives as a result of a family dispute over inheritance. The man, it would appear, had no connection whatsoever to either the victim or the crime.

Raymond Downing, Stephen's father, was a suspect in name only because he had been driving the bus which dropped Wendy Sewell near her workplace on the morning she was assaulted. There was no credible reason why he should be considered a suspect. Raymond Downing's elimination from the investigation was entirely correct.

There is no doubt that Wendy Sewell had a somewhat liberal lifestyle, to put it politely. Some sections of the media in recent years have put it less politely, nicknaming her the 'Bakewell Tart'. Although she was married she had a string of lovers and a penchant for outdoor sex. She had given birth to a child from one of her many boyfriends, whilst married to her husband David. That child had been adopted and the father could have been any one of three men.

Wendy would use her generous two-hour lunch breaks for sexual rendezvous at the cemetery where she was killed. Her liaisons were no secret. Her lifestyle was a source of gossip and well known in the close-knit community.

Her marriage to David Sewell had been turbulent, with the couple often breaking up. At one point Wendy had moved into a flat above a shop only to be asked to leave due to the frequent visits from a wide range of men.

By the time of Wendy's death, however, the couple had begun to patch their relationship back together and were living in the same house. Nonetheless, it has been suggested that her extra-marital affairs continued and that indeed she decided to meet a lover at the cemetery on that tragic autumn day.

When she left for lunch on the day of her fatal attack, Wendy left a note for her boss saying she had gone 'for a breath of fresh air'. There was no mention of her going to look at gravestones. It is not in dispute that the note was indeed penned by Wendy Sewell.

Her boss has, in recent years, allegedly spoken of overhearing a conversation between Wendy and another individual at Noon on the day of the attack. The boss was in the next room and could apparently hear Wendy's raised voice but no one else. It was assumed the conversation was on the telephone and it is believed that it was a boyfriend she was talking to. Then, just under forty minutes later, Wendy left and was allegedly seen

looking excited and indicated to a colleague that she was meeting her boyfriend to reconcile with him.

A witness came forward after Downing was convicted claiming she had not only seen Wendy Sewell alive at a time when Downing had an alibi, but that she also saw the victim walking around the cemetery kissing a man. She described the man as having sandy-coloured, shoulder-length hair, wearing a denim jacket and jeans. Her claims were dismissed because it was said there were trees partially obstructing her view of the cemetery and also she was short sighted and so could not give an accurate identification of who she saw. Even so, who was that man? Was he involved in the murder or could he have been a witness? The man has never come forward.

The police looked into all of the claims relating to Wendy being killed by alleged lovers and found no evidence to substantiate them. Those involved in Downing's campaign, however, have argued that there is too much fear amongst certain witnesses to tell the truth to the police because the real killer still lives locally. Detectives dismiss such claims.

Police door-to-door enquiries during the Operation Noble revealed that a man allegedly confessed to murdering Wendy Sewell. The alleged witness to the confession and the individual who is claimed to have said he battered the typist, were both questioned. Detectives were satisfied to eliminate the man from their investigation.

The victim's husband, David Sewell has been a popular suspect amongst many who have studied the case. He was, however, at work in Derby and received a telephone call at work, from the police to inform him of the assault on his wife, a short time after the attack. The police have always been satisfied of his innocence.

A witness alleged to have seen a bloodstained man running very quickly as if he was in a hurry, up Yeld Road towards Lady Manners School away from the cemetery. The witness identified the man, who was not Stephen Downing, seeing a photograph of him in the *Derbyshire Times* newspaper in 1974. Years later she claimed the man was wearing bloodstained clothing, though there was no mention of blood in her police statements or trial testimony. Another witness saw a 'hurrying

man' running on Upper Yeld Road in the direction of the school and later saw a man who he believed was the same man, outside the school. The descriptions from the two witnesses, however, differ greatly. It is known that a man, quite innocently used to jog home along this route every lunchtime for his lunch. This may account for one of the witnesses' sightings, but if two men were seen then who was the second man and why was he in such a rush? Neither man could have been Downing.

An anonymous letter was presented to the police during their reinvestigation. The author of the letter claimed to have heard shouting at the cemetery on the day Wendy Sewell was attacked before seeing a man running from the scene of the crime. After seeing the man run away the writer, believed to be a woman, claimed to then witness Stephen Downing entering the cemetery. Without knowing the identity of the author, and questioning that individual, it is impossible to assign any credibility or significance to the letter. It could have been written for a variety of motives. The author of the letter had not come forward, she said, because she was in the woods next to the cemetery meeting a lover who was not her husband.

According to Don Hale a man, dubbed 'Mr I' by detectives, had boasted about 'finishing Wendy Sewell off' following the attack. When questioned by police as part of Operation Noble the source of Hale's information denied having heard such boasts. Detectives were happy to eliminate Mr I when they discovered he was at work at the time of the attack.

Another anonymous letter sent to Bakewell Police Station in October 2001 identified the killer as a man named 'Mr K'. The author of the letter, who alleges he or she was dying of a terminal illness, maintains that Mr K confessed to the murder during a drunken rage. When questioned by detectives Mr K denied ever having claimed responsibility for Wendy Sewell's death and claimed he did not know her, a claim which police investigations support. Mr K was unsure about his movements on the day of the attack but the police were satisfied of his innocence.

A friend of Wendy's informed police officers that a man used to invite himself into the victim's home when she lived at Wyedale Crescent, Bakewell prior to 1971 when she moved to

Youlgreave. The man, upon being questioned by detectives, denied this. Detectives were unable to find any evidence linking the man to the murder.

As part of the police reinvestigation, Downing was for obvious reasons a suspect and so the police were keen to speak to him to discuss a number of issues, some of which I will now detail.

Since Stephen Downing's release from prison he has made a number of confessions to the murder of Wendy Sewell. A woman he was in a relationship with after his release taped him confessing during an argument. He is also alleged to have confessed to his father in April 2002 and on a later occasion.

Downing maintains that the confessions were not genuine, adding that the taped confession was his attempt to tell his then girlfriend what he thought she wanted to hear, saying words to the effect of 'If you want to think that I did it, then yes I did it.'

Following his conviction, Downing claimed that he had seen two men at the cemetery whilst attending to Wendy as she lay injured. Apparently one of the men had told him that if he turned round he and his sister would be assaulted. The police would have liked to have discussed this alleged incident with Downing because no statement was ever given by him regarding it.

The police also wished to discuss whether Downing had sexually assaulted Wendy Sewell, even if he had not murdered her, despite no evidence of a sexual assault having taken place. The likelihood of a murderer and sex attacker being in the same cemetery at the same time seems rather remote.

It is unfortunate that Downing refused to be formally interviewed once again in connection to the aforementioned issues, on the advice of his legal team. Whilst he did cooperate with the reinvestigation, his decision meant that he could not be eliminated from the police enquiries and it has ensured that there will always be some doubts lingering over whether he should have been released. If he was innocent, it will also reinforce the police's belief that they have identified Wendy Sewell's killer and will mean that the case will not be reopened unless significant new evidence is forthcoming. The police

report concluded: 'In the absence of an interview with Stephen Downing and the opportunity to independently fully assess these issues, it is not possible to eliminate Stephen Downing from the enquiry... The police are not looking for any other person for the murder of Wendy Sewell, a young woman in the prime of her life who was robbed of her future as a result of this vicious attack. All possible lines of enquiry have been exhausted. The case is now closed unless any substantial new evidence comes to light.'

The police were wrong to say this. All possible lines of enquiry have not been exhausted. The police have still not traced the man and woman seen embracing in the cemetery. The police have still not traced and investigated the man seen running up Yeld Road following the crime. They have still not traced the person that Wendy was talking to before she left work or determined who she was intending to meet. The police also have forensic evidence relating to the murder, evidence that has never been examined using modern techniques. They have the murder weapon complete with unidentified prints and bloodstaining from two individuals; the victim and some other unknown person who was not Stephen Downing. Was the blood from Wendy's killer? We have already learnt that only Wendy's DNA was found on the murder weapon, despite there being blood from two people, but there is the potential to identify the killer's DNA from other sources.

Wendy struggled with her attacker and scratched him. She was conscious throughout the violent attack upon her. Stephen Downing had no scratches or injuries, but there was skin under Wendy's fingernails. The skin was not that of Stephen Downing. Could it have been from her killer? Given that Wendy died as a result of a frenzied attack before being partially stripped, there is every possibility that her killer left DNA on her clothing. It is true that some contamination of exhibits has taken place but advanced scientific methods such as Low Copy Number DNA analysis can identify even the smallest traces of DNA, even if only one or two cells are present. There is plenty of scope for forensic analysis to identify through scientific techniques, Wendy Sewell's murderer. The police just require the will to undertake the tests. As a result of Stephen Downing's

appeal in 2002 not being contested by the prosecution, many pieces of new evidence were never fully examined in court but if the murderer of Wendy Sewell is ever to be brought to justice, those pieces of evidence, particularly the forensic evidence, must be fully examined and suspects eliminated accordingly.

The case has led to all manner of conspiracy theories and the police have done nothing to prevent these theories from gaining popularity. Operation Noble, despite the amount of resources provided to the reinvestigation, failed to address all of the issues. Also, my own research has revealed that the report of the Director of Public Prosecution in relation to Stephen Downing has been made exempt from the Freedom of Information Act for a period of ninety-five years, begging the question of what is contained in that report that warrants it to be kept from public view. If the investigation is closed why are the police reluctant to release any of the information contained within the file?

Whatever people think about the case of Stephen Downing, Wendy Sewell's killer is not serving a sentence for her murder and the police are not absolutely sure as to who was responsible for battering the young woman to death in 1973. Her murder remains unsolved and thirty-six years after her death it is quite likely that the violent killer is still alive and free.

CHAPTER 13

Elaine Wakefield: Axe Edge, Buxton

1982

Ｎews of a fatal sex crime began to spread through the small town of Buxton on the afternoon of Saturday 27 February 1982, leaving the residents in a state of shock and horror. At half past two on that afternoon a motorcyclist making his way through mist and rain to the High Edge Raceway, Axe Edge, six miles south of the Derbyshire town, had stumbled across a disturbing sight.

As he approached the raceway, where preparations were to be made for a race meeting, he noticed something inside the fencing of the compound that did not look right. Looking closer it soon became apparent that it was the body of a young dead woman. The body was only partially clothed, wearing only a bra. The remainder of her clothing was found scattered two hundred yards away.

The raceway was located on moorland and was rarely used during weekdays, making it in an ideal spot for courting couples.

The body was that of Elaine Irene Wakefield, a twenty-year-old woman originally from Tunstead Milton, where she continued to work as a petrol pump attendant, but had moved to Buxton to live with her boyfriend. She had last been seen on Thursday 25 February and all of the evidence has pointed to her having been killed on that Thursday afternoon.

A post-mortem examination revealed that Elaine had died quickly after a relatively minor compression of a nerve in her neck. It was believed the injury was consistent with autoerotic asphyxiation, where someone places their hands around a partner's neck during sex, to reduce their partners intake of oxygen, in order to heighten sexual pleasure. Only a fairly small

amount of force was exerted by the killer in order to carry out his crime.

An inquest into the death would later record an open verdict, with the realisation there was no evidence to conclusively disprove the possibility that Elaine was the victim of a sex game that went wrong, but detectives investigating the death believed it was a case of murder. This was despite the fact the police publicly claimed, in the local press, that Elaine had died as a result of 'horseplay', with her killer being taken 'completely by surprise and panic'. The fact is she engaged in some sexual activity with her killer, either of her own free will or as a result of force, and at some point she lost her life and her killer left and failed to come forward. Elaine either died in a vehicle and was semi-clothed or her killer removed her clothing after death, possibly pointing to a degree of premeditation. It was likely the murderer did have a car. There was no evidence to prove Elaine was killed where her body was found, although the fact she was seen walking in that direction suggests she probably was killed at the High Edge Raceway, or nearby.

There were no clues at the scene to help identify the killer, though DNA would be found on Elaine's clothing more than two decades later. A thorough search of the area only located four Second World War unexploded bombs. Detectives soon confirmed that soldiers had been working in the area, in the week before Elaine's murder, carrying out bomb disposal work; the area had been used for storing bombs during the war but none of the soldiers could shed any light on the tragedy.

Local people each provided separate sightings of the deceased, which enabled detectives to reconstruct Elaine's movements. Elaine was five foot two inches, of 'plump' build, with blue eyes and short light brown cropped hair. On the day she died she had been wearing blue denim jeans, with a red and yellow patch on the right knee, a brown quilted zip up anorak and tan shoes.

A police reconstruction was staged in order to try and obtain further witnesses who may have seen Elaine on her final walk and, hopefully, might have seen her killer. A twenty-one-year-old civilian police typist based at Buxton Police Station was chosen to act as Elaine. Dawn Hadfield walked part of the

route detectives believed the victim walked, wearing identical clothing to that worn by Elaine.

Elaine had been seen at nine different points along her journey and there was no dispute that the sightings were of the right person. It was determined she had left her flat at 51 West Road, Buxton, on the afternoon of Thursday 25 February, walked along the A6 from Buxton, being seen at between 2pm and 2.30pm at traffic lights near the Bakewell Road/Dale Road junction, before heading on to Duke's Drive to join the A515 South to Brierlow Bar, where she turned right on to a small road in the direction of Earl Sterndale before taking a second right on to a back road leading to the raceway. In total it was a seven mile walk which, it was believed, would have taken Elaine around two hours to complete. There was no evidence of her having tried, or succeeded, in hitching a lift, with the information provided by the local residents suggesting she probably arrived at the raceway on her own, though the possibility that Elaine got a lift part of the way to the raceway could never be totally ruled out. There was no evidence that she was followed.

The weather that afternoon became increasingly hostile, with temperatures low enough for the roads to have started to become icy as Elaine walked, and fog falling over the area. It was also damp and there was a little snow in the air. Nonetheless, detectives did not believe there was anything strange about her walking to the raceway in those conditions. 'It was not unusual for her to walk long distances,' Detective Superintendent Naylor said.

The police have always believed that Elaine was intending to meet someone and that that man could very well have been her killer. 'There could have been an arranged meeting with someone – I would expect it to be male. All her boyfriends are being seen,' the press was told.

Elaine had been up to the raceway with a boyfriend in the past but the police did not believe she went there with the intention of meeting someone for sex, despite the reputation the area had at that time. It does seem a rather unusual place to meet someone for just a casual conversation and whilst Elaine may have been the type of woman who did not mind

walking long distances in bad weather, as far as I am concerned it would be stretching the limit of probability to suggest that she walked through adverse weather conditions, to a remote spot for something other than a sexual rendezvous or romantic encounter. Somebody lured her to that spot and that individual can only be the one whose hands ultimately cut her life short.

Elaine's boyfriend was a married serving police constable, aged thirty-three. After his girlfriend's death he became a suspect but no evidence was uncovered to show he was the killer, though he was not eliminated from the investigation at that time. Questions about his possible involvement in his girlfriend's death were inevitable and were a source of much gossip among sections of the community. These stories no doubt played a major role in his decision to leave the police force and emigrate. However, in recent years the former officer has been questioned once again and gave a DNA sample. He was eliminated from the investigation but despite conclusive proof of his innocence, some of the gossip mongerers continue to this day to share their erroneous beliefs.

Detective Superintendent Tom Naylor, who led the original hunt for Elaine's killer, was convinced the person he sought was a local man: 'The inquiry is local,' he told the *Buxton Advertiser* in March 1982 before asking for anyone with knowledge of 'a relative, friend or acquaintance who has acted strangely, or has appeared in any way worried or depressed by the incident' to get in touch with the police.

Although it was always believed the individual responsible for murdering Elaine was a local man, the possibility he lived outside the area should never have been ignored. Buxton is a small town and Elaine did not have a lifestyle that necessitated her to travel very far. It was for this reason that the police assumed the killer must have lived close to the Derbyshire town. It is dangerous to make such assumptions because in doing so detectives closed their minds to other possibilities and indeed the possibility that Elaine was killed by someone who was not local is actually very strong indeed.

Elaine was a keen CB radio enthusiast and detectives are now considering the possibility she met her killer by talking to him via her CB; used by many as an earlier equivalent to the internet

chat room. If this was the case the police may have made a major error in concentrating their resources on a small area when he could conceivably have lived in any part of the country where the range of Elaine's CB covered. Nonetheless, it is probable her killer knew the area relatively well in order for him to locate the raceway, though it cannot be ruled out that he could have found this information without previously visiting Buxton or having visited the area before the crime in order to become familiar with it. The police's original assertion it was a local investigation may very well have jeopardised their chance of success.

A tall man, probably wearing red, was seen jogging along the Ashbourne Road on the afternoon of 25 February, the day on which Elaine was last seen alive. However, the High Peak Half-Marathon was held on the Sunday of that week and so he may not have been involved in the crime; he might simply have been training for the race. Nonetheless he never came forward and could potentially have provided the police with important information. Other than the colour of part of his clothing and the fact he was tall, nothing is known about this man. People run along roads for a variety of reasons, both innocent and sinister in their nature. Besides, there is every chance that the man responsible drove away from the scene of the crime, especially if he was someone who had met Elaine following a conversation with her over the airwaves.

During the original investigation more than 1,000 enquiries were made and 737 statements were written. Yet despite huge resources being spent on this murder hunt, the police came no closer to learning the truth about the identity of Elaine's killer. The passage of time has not, however, prevented the police from wishing to bring the killer to justice. In October 2003, Derbyshire Constabulary reopened the case in the hope that new forensic techniques could help them catch the man they have sought for more than two decades.

Each of the original suspects was asked to supply a sample of DNA after forensic examination of Elaine's clothing revealed a small amount of DNA which could have originated from her killer. None of those who could be traced provided DNA matching the murderer's and they were all eliminated following

decades of suspicion hanging over them. Following a public appeal through television, radio and press reports, detectives announced they had received several 'interesting calls' from members of the public, but none were able to lead to a successful conclusion. 'There has been a surprisingly good response from the public, and while we have not been inundated, most of the calls and letters we have received have been quite focussed and informative and have not been a waste of time. I am very grateful people are responding to the appeal, but I'm sure there is a lot more information out there which is relevant to this inquiry', detectives told the media in the hope of finding crucial information that could nail Elaine's killer. That information is still elusive.

Detective Superintendent Malcolm Parkin, who is leading the new hunt for Elaine's killer, offers hope for those seeking justice for Elaine and other victims of unsolved murders: 'The files on undetected murders are never closed. Improvements in investigation techniques and DNA analysis mean forces can look at old cases with fresh eyes,' he told the media.

We can only hope that one day someone in the Derbyshire Constabulary will be able to look with fresh eyes at this mystery and find a solution to who killed Elaine Wakefield on that February day in 1982, and why her life was untimely ended. Until that day, the case remains as cold as the afternoon on which Elaine's life was tragically cut short. Even with the most advanced forensic science techniques available to police forces, and with detectives far better equipped and experienced than their counterparts earlier in the twentieth century, some murderers still have luck on their side. With increased awareness of the unsolved crimes of the past, murderers should have renewed fear and resume looking over their shoulders. New police efforts with public cooperation should never be underestimated and a killer's luck can always run out. Let us hope this is the case for Elaine Wakefield and the other unfortunate victims of unsolved murders in and around Derbyshire.

Bibliography

Mexican Joe
Burton Daily Mail, various between 29 November and throughout December 1908.
Nutt, G, 1996, *A Stranger, A Ghost, & A Conjuror*, the Magic Attic.

Clara Durose
Burton Daily Mail, 5 April 1910
Burton Daily Mail, 6 April 1910
The Burton Chronicle, 7 April 1910
Burton Daily Mail, 8 April 1910
Burton Daily Mail, 22 April 1910
Burton Daily Mail, 10 May 1910
Burton Daily Mail, 25 May 1910
Burton Daily Mail, 26 May 1910
Burton Daily Mail, 27 May 1910
Burton Daily Mail, 30 May 1910

Thomas Ward
The Derbyshire Advertiser, 10 June 1921
Derby Mercury, 17 June 1921
Derby Mercury, 24 June 1921
The Derbyshire Advertiser, 24 June 1921
The Derbyshire Advertiser, 8 July 1921
The Derbyshire Advertiser, 18 November 1921

Samuel Fell Wilson
Nottingham Evening Post, 23 September 1930
Nottingham Journal, 24 September 1930
Nottingham Evening Post, 25 September 1930
Nottingham Evening Post, 26 September 1930
Nottingham Evening Post, 27 September 1930
Nottingham Evening Post, 29 September 1930

Nottingham Evening Post, 30 September 1930
Nottingham Evening Post, 1 October 1930
Nottingham Evening Post, 17 October 1930

George Harry Tyler
Burton Daily Mail, 30 April 1947
Burton Daily Mail, 1 May 1947
The Times, 2 May 1947
Burton Daily Mail, 2 May 1947
Burton Daily Mail, 3 May 1947

George Wilson
The Times, 9 September 1963
The Times, 10 September 1963
The Times, 12 September 1963
The Times, 16 September 1963
The Times, 23 December 1963
The Times, 6 December 1965
The Nottingham Journal, 7 March 1973
Nottingham Evening Post, 13 February 1984

Mavis Hudson
The Derbyshire Times, 6 January 1967
The Times, 28 December 1966
The Times, 2 January 1967

Victim Unknown
Burton Mail, 27 March 1971
Burton Mail, 29 March 1971

Annie Walker
Leicester Mercury, 3 April 1969
Leicester Mercury, 4 April 1969
Leicester Mercury, 5 April 1969
Leicester Mercury, 12 April 1969
Leicester Mercury, 14 April 1969
Leicester Mercury, 20 April 1969
Leicester Mercury, 21 April 1969
BBC News website, 18 October 2005

Barbara Mayo
The Times, 20 October 1970
The Derbyshire Times, 23 October 1970
Mid Cheshire Guardian, 26 September 1997
BBC News website, 4 January 1999
Mid Cheshire Guardian, 1 February 1999
The Observer, 18 November 2007
Liverpool Daily Post, 24 May 2008

Judith Roberts
Court of Appeal Judgment: Evans, R v [1997] EWCA Crim
    3145 (3 December 1997)
BBC News website Wednesday 3 December 1997

Wendy Sewell
BBC News website, 18 August 2000
Hale, D, Huns, M and McGregor, H., 2002, *A Town Without
    Pity* (London: Time Warner Books UK).
Derbyshire Constabulary, 2002, *Operation Noble: The Police
    Reinvestigation of the Murder of Wendy Sewell*
Court of Appeal Judgment: Downing, R v [2002] EWCA Crim
    263 (15 January 2002)

Elaine Wakefield
Buxton Advertiser, 4 March 1982
Buxton Advertiser, 11 March 1982
BBC news website, 2 October 2003
Manchester Evening News, 3 October 2003
Buxton Advertiser, 10 November 2003

Index